"Coward"

"Coward's War"

The Diaries of Private George H Coward
Somerset Light Infantry and Royal Engineers

An "Old Contemptible's" view of the Great War

edited by
Tim Machin

Matador
9 De Montfort Mews
Leicester LE1 7FW, UK
Tel: (+44) 116 255 9311 / 9312
Email: books@troubador.co.uk
Web: www.troubador.co.uk/matador

ISBN 10: 1-905886-13-6
ISBN 13: 978-1-905886-13-5

Typeset in 12pt Bembo by Troubador Publishing Ltd, Leicester, UK
Printed in the UK by The Cromwell Press Ltd, Trowbridge, Wilts, UK

Matador is an imprint of Troubador Publishing Ltd

To Irene [née Coward] and Donald Martin

Contents

Acknowledgements

To Nic Cox for his help in unscrambling the diaries.

The Great War Forum and Chris Baker for permission to use maps found on their excellent website.

Tonie and Valmai Holt for permission to use the Bairnsfather cartoon.

Lothian Health Trust for permission to use photographs of the Deaconess Hospital, Edinburgh.

Irene and Donald Martin for extra information about George Coward.

The National Archive for permission to use the 1901 census return and the medal document.

The Scotsman for permission to use extracts from their archives.

Somerset County Records Office for permission to use some photos relating to the Somerset Light Infantry.

Preface

For 35 years I taught History at Bedford School, and the curriculum usually contained some aspect of the Great War, be it at IB level or with junior classes. Each year a "Trenches Trip" was organised for 50 or so 13 to 14 year olds, and each year this visit to Ypres and the Somme left an indelible mark on them all.

Some time before I retired I was given a photocopy of the diaries of a soldier who fought through and survived the 1914-18 War. They lay in my desk for a few years, but I determined to do something about them when I had more time, and so I started work on them in September 2005, following my retirement in the summer of that year.

The first problem was to find out whose diaries they were, as at no stage did they reveal the surname, though I came to find out his first name was George! I wanted to contact his family, if possible, to find out more about him, to tell them of my project, and to get their permission to try and publish the remarkable documents I had in my possession.

On the first page of his diaries he mentioned that he was invalided from the Ypres Salient to a hospital in Edinburgh in early November 1914. Whilst there he was interviewed by a journalist from the *Scotsman*, and the reporter looked at the diaries that the soldier had kept concerning the first few months of the War. I looked at the archives of the *Scotsman*, and there, on November 4th 1914, appeared an article concerning this, and from this I was able to find out both the name of the Regiment the soldier belonged to, and also his name. He was George Henry Coward, who was in the Somerset Light Infantry.

After that things slowly fell into place, and from the photocopied diaries I could work out his age and where he came from.

George was born in Bath in 1888, joined the Army for the first time in

1906, was married in 1914, and he had 3 children, Irene born in 1914, Lionel born in 1916, and Vera born in 1920. I found this out using the 1901 census that is available on the Internet, and the various Ancestral Search firms that were online [at a price!]. I could not, however, get past the year 1959, and I wanted to get right up to date with present relations. I contacted everyone called Coward who lived in the Bath region and had some interesting replies in their own right, but could not get to the right family. But, by further searching I was able to find the death certificate of Lionel who died in Bournemouth in 1997, and which was signed by his sister, Irene. This was the breakthrough! I managed to find Irene Coward, the soldier's daughter, who now resided near Newbury, and who is now into her nineties. I went to visit her in early January 2006.

We were both very pleased, I because of being able to find her and talk to her, and she, because of the rediscovery of her Father's diaries.

We agreed that I should try and get them published, and essentially what I have done is editing and adding some context, by the means of endnotes, to the fascinating tales of an Old Contemptible, who fought on the Somme, at Ypres, at Arras, on the Marne and Aisne, and whose story in the early part of the war began with the Retreat from Mons.

Moreover he writes about being in the peacetime army between 1906-13, and on life as a civilian in Bath and Bristol both before and immediately after World War One. He, like so many other former soldiers, failed to find the Brave New World that was promised.

George died in 1962. A fascinating "coincidence", is that an occupant of the house where he was born in 1888, was killed in the "Bath Blitz" of the Second World War. Also that when he was demobbed from the RE in 1919 in Bedford, he was living in a house not 100 yards from where I am writing this!

As with so many records of war, these diaries show the interaction of an "ordinary" citizen with the extraordinary events of the Great War. As ever, human spirit rises to the surface!

Tim Machin
MA Oxon

Introduction

The diaries begin thus.

Deaconess Hospital, Edinburgh November 1914

In November 1914, I was laying in hospital in Edinburgh, recovering from the effects of being blown up by one of Fritz's big shells out in "Plug-Street"[1] Wood, Belgium. One day, whilst in hospital, a reporter of the *Scotsman*, an Edinburgh newspaper, visited the ward seeking "pretty stories" of the war. Going from one cot to another all around the ward he eventually arrived at my cot and asked me if I had any stories to relate. Now I had kept a rough diary of what I had been through in France and Belgium during the last 3 months so I offered the diary to him to do as he liked with. On his reading it through he decided it would make a good story and so he copied it in his own book in shorthand. Well now he sent me a copy of the *Scotsman* when it appeared – November 4th 1914 – and my bit of news did look rather pretty so I decided to carry on keeping a diary and one day re-write it all through, and try to get it published.

Wounded arriving and being tended at Deaconess Hospital

The images of the Deaconess Hospital, Edinburgh are reproduced by kind permission of the Lothian Health Services Archive, Edinburgh University Library.

A SOLDIER'S DIARY

WITH THE SOMERSETS IN BELGIUM.

Among the forty soldiers who are being attended to in the Deaconess Hospital, Edinburgh, is Private Coward, of the Somersets. Private Coward went out to France with his regiment in the early days of the war, and kept a rough diary of the incidents which filled in the days from the time of embarkation until the 31st of last month, when he was put out of action by the bursting of a heavy German shell. The diary, roughly written in an old note-book in pencil, was not intended for publication. It traces the retreat from Mons, the fighting on the Marne, which marked the "turning of the tide," the siege warfare of the Aisne, and, latterly, the fierce engagements on the French frontier and in Belgium. Some extracts are given:—

August 25.—Very stiff work and long marches. Rested outside a village near St Saviour, near Compiègne Forest. General Hunter Weston came back and said, "There's a chance here to get your own back, lads." A number of German cavalry were in front, cut off from the main body. Had a nice little scrap with some Uhlans, and smashed them completely. Four shrapnel shells dropped just in the rear of us. Didn't know they had guns with them. Found out later that it was only the mist that saved us from being wiped out.

AGAINST HEAVY ODDS.

October 16.—Slept in an infant school. Moved out in the early morning and attacked. A and B Companies were together. Very hot time. Germans were strongly entrenched, and we had to go over the open. We had our bayonets fixed. When they saw us coming they ran for it. About 80 came towards us with their hands up. They had thrown away their rifles. Our chaps were chasing others with the bayonet. Captured 39 and killed heaps. Our big guns got splendid range of them, and finished off those we couldn't reach as they retired into a wood. Were told by our C.O. that our two companies had killed and captured 450. In all 1400 were killed, captured, and wounded. We lost only a few men. In this fight we were 450 against something like 4500.

October 20.—Amusing incident. The Q.M.S. said he knew the way to the trenches in the dark with the rations. The men believed him, and he took them to the German trenches instead. He was captured with the rations. Good for the Germans, but our boys had to go without the rations.

NIGHT ATTACKS.

October 22.—Were moved up at night to relieve Hants, who were in position in the trenches about two miles on our left front. Told us they had been there two days and two nights. We thought we would get relieved, but had to stick it a bit. Almost as soon as we were in position we were attacked, twice in the night of the 22nd and at dawn on the 23rd. Kept our positions.

October 24.—Told that a general advance by enemy was expected. Warned to keep a sharp lookout.

October 25.—Nothing special happened during the day except for continual sniping all along the line, which made it dangerous to get out of the trenches. As night fell it came on heavy rain. Most uncomfortable night since the war began. About 9 P.M. the enemy attacked. Never had such a night in my life. Beat them back. Never fired so many rounds before. It was the same all along the line. The attack was expected, and everybody was ready.

October 25.— Very quiet all day and night. Enemy set fire to a church on our left with shell fire, and made it light as day. This made it impossible for us to attack without being seen. When there is no moon they usually give us a bonfire.

MORE WOUNDED SOLDIERS IN EDINBURGH

A further batch of wounded soldiers belonging to the British Expeditionary Force arrived in the Caledonian Station, Edinburgh, yesterday forenoon from Southampton. About 150 men were on the hospital train, which arrived between nine and ten o'clock. As usual, there was an adequate Red Cross staff in waiting, and the task of conveying the wounded men to hospital was carried through smoothly and swiftly. There were twenty somewhat serious cases, and these men were removed in motor ambulances, but the others were able, in some instances with a little assistance, to walk to the motor cars, of which a large number had been placed at the disposal of the Red Cross officials. Forty of the men were accommodated in the Church of Scotland Deaconess Hospital, and the remainder were taken to Craigleith Military Hospital. Very few of the soldiers belong to Scottish regiments. They have been engaged in the hard fighting which has been taking place on the Belgian frontier. Despite their wounds most of the soldiers were in excellent spirits. There was one veteran who had seen 37 years' continuous service; 19 of which had been spent in India.

WOUNDED AT DEACONESS HOSPITAL.

Forty wounded soldiers were taken to the Deaconess Hospital. This is the first occasion on which wounded soldiers of the Expeditionary Force have been accommodated in the Church of Scotland hospital in the Pleasance, where the normal accommodation has been increased in order to meet the present emergency. The names of the soldiers are as follows:—

6146 Pte. Daniel Cahill, Royal Irish Regt.
9028 Gen. Henry Bell, 1st Wilts Regt.
11945 Sapper Sydney Painter, Royal Engineers.
8179 Pte. Harry Rogers, Duke of Cornwall's Light Infantry.
7757 Pte. Albert Gillett, 1st Wilts Regt.
7183 L.-C. Sidney Norris, 1st Wilts Regt.
9726 Pte. Wm. Lowe, 1st Buffs.
7181 Pte. Frank Horrell, 1st Wilts Regt.
8245 Bandsman Harry Cosgrove, Connaught Rangers.
7465 Pte. John Hagne, 1st South Staffords.
6887 Pte. Fred. Luckman, 1st Wilts Regt.
6881 Pte. Lewis Gilligan.

8802 Pte. Thos. Morris, 1st South Staffords.
10238 Pte. James Williamson, 2nd Royal Irish Rifles.
15474 Pte. Alfred Cox, 4th Royal Fusiliers.
6164 Pte. H. G. Cooper, 1st Wilts Regt.
8118 L.-C. G. H. Simms, 1st Duke of Cornwall's Light Infantry.
6967 Pte. H. T. Candy, 1st Wilts Regt.
8724 Pte. Alfred Pardoe, 1st South Staffords.
4372 Pte. J. Hamilton, 1st Irish Guards.
7085 Pte. John Wyne, 2nd Royal Irish Rifles.
8010 Pte. Geo. Coward, 1st Somersets.
6943 Pte. Jos. M'Quide, 1st Northumberland F.
4158 Pte. Arthur Hodson.

Extracts that appeared in the Scotsman *on November 4 1914*
Reproduced with the kind permission of the *Scotsman* 2006.

Bath 1906

Well. Reader, I've done the job at last and I'm letting you see now how, why, and wherefore "your humble servant" became an "Old Contemptible". I have to go back a few years reader, and that won't hurt so much, it's the going forward a few years that most of us dread. However, away back a pal and I thought we would like to see life, and being young'uns that had no troubles or worries we went on "shanks pony" several times to Bristol and Avonmouth just to have a look at the ships. I well remember the visions I used to conjure up of stowing away aboard some of those sailing vessels that I've seen lying alongside the quay down in Bristol, and well remember getting a wet mop flung at me when I and my pal tried to get aboard one day.

It is suggested that you read the summary of the action of The Somerset Light Infantry that is on pages 186–189 before setting out on the book. Private Coward's career in the 1st World War, as described in his diaries, keeps almost perfect synchronisation with the Summary until he transfers to the Royal Engineers as a specialist Signaller on May 29 1917.

CHAPTER I

The Somerset Light Infantry 1906–13

'Signing up'

Well, as our luck was out at that game (stowing away by ship), we decided to see the world in another fashion. So, returning to our native town, Bath, we took the plunge into the arms of an old recruiting sergeant, and, after a general overhaul we were passed as "fit to go" a serving of His Majesty, as Kipling said. Thus, at the age of 18 years and 3 months in October 1906 I found myself starting on my career, which was to bring me out as an "Old Contemptible"[2].

The Sergeant saw myself and my pal onto the train and away to Taunton where they filed the rough lumps off us. I might say that my pal was not passed as fit to go straight into the regular army until he had been "pulled together" by serving 6 months in the Militia, but I went straight away. Well it will not be of interest to you to know the rigmarole of licking a "Tommy" into shape, so I'll just say that I passed out as fit to join the regiment at the end of January 1907, and I came home on my first Depot leave for Christmas '06 [a full blown recruit].

I joined the regiment at Crown Hill Barracks in January 1907, and went to good old 7th Coy for Company Training, Battalion Training, Brigade Training, Manoeuvres [on Salisbury Plain], and a 3 months course of "Mounted Infantry" at Longmoor Camp, Hampshire, to say nothing of "gun firing courses", route marches and Sergeant-Major Parades.

These soon made me feel as though this was the life to lead. The weeks and months slipping by, I find myself into January 1908 before I can say

The Somerset Light Infantry in camp on Salisbury Plain

"Jack Robinson". I now had my second furlough, which was of 6 weeks duration, so that early in January 1908 I find myself on my way down to Mutley station, Plymouth, en route for Bath and her "beauties", [there are also some "beauties" in Plymouth by the way].

Well I arrived in Bath this time [a full blown private], "passed out" in everything, even to the noble art of playing "banker" at Sling Plantation, a military camp on Salisbury Plain. Of course I was "in" as we all were when we came on furlough, having plenty of money, nothing to do but strut around and spend it on fags, theatres and palaces and such like, and then away back to Plymouth to earn some more. The same sort of thing had to be undertaken again as regards training and such like, bringing us around to June 1908 when the regiment was ordered to go "under canvas" for a month on the moors behind Plymouth. We were camped at a place called Willsworthy, and after a month we received orders that we were to march so many miles a day to Salisbury Plain. I know I've heard of Napoleon's, or some other chaps, retreat from Moscow, and I've also heard of someone else's march from Kabul to Kandahar, but I don't reckon they had much to grouse about. The one from Moscow was done in the snow, and the other from Kabul must have been done in the heat, and ours was done in a mixture of both. Still it all went towards us being as fit as fiddles, and we arrived at Larkhill Camp one day after, I believe, about 12 days trekking. We had then near enough a month's manoeuvres and then got the news that the regiment was under orders for Malta.

Malta

We finished manoeuvres and entrained to Plymouth once more and then all were given 6 weeks leave, and were due back about the 20th October 1908. Well now after getting served out with helmet, overseas kit, and "several thousand" inspections that had to be gone through, we find ourselves on our way down to Keyham Docks [Devonport] to embark. All the way down through the streets, flags and streamers were flying about, bands playing, women crying [what for I dunno, unless some of them were married and were crying for joy to see the backs of their "old men" for a few years]. What the fuss was all about I don't know, as we young'uns were highly amused to think we were off to see the world. By now I had had 2 years service, and, of course, I had plenty of new found chums. Chums mind, real chums, not like the ones you find in "civvy" life. [You find heaps of chums in "civvy" life as long as you are "mended", but few when you are broke.]

However we find ourselves embarking on the *SS Rohilla*[3] [a transport that went down off Whitby during the war], and on the afternoon of Friday November 5th 1908 we steamed out of Plymouth Sound to the tunes of "Auld Lang's Syne", "The girl I left behind me", and "Will ye no come back again?". We're off to see the world and as it was getting dusk we saw the light of Eddystone winking and blinking at us. It seemed to be saying "you lucky devils". The Bay of Biscay was not very kind to us, but without boasting, I can truthfully say, I've never yet been seasick, but some of my old pals had a terrible time before we reached Gibraltar. I remember a chum called Macdonald from London [a London Jock] saying to me, "George, I've brought up my breakfast, I've brought up my dinner, and I'm waiting now for my tea to come back up, and then I'm going to lie down and pray for the Lord to knock a damned [or worse] hole in the ship". Poor old Mac, he was in a fix. Either he did not pray, or else the Lord was not listening, as we passed Gib by night and kept our course for Malta, where we arrived in glorious sunshine on November 12th.

A coincidence about it was that we were on one boat, a battalion just out from England, and next day the old transport, *Plassey*, came in with our other battalion from India on her way to Portland. So we had two battalions of one regiment in Malta Harbour at the same time. As soon as we pulled in around the Fliemar Creek under Fort Manuel, we were promptly surrounded by a host of small boats selling fruit and all sorts of tackle. We had orders to get ready for disembarking which did not take long once it started, but was hard work in the head on "baggage fatigue". After a few days we were soon settled down in Floriana Barracks, and one day a notice was posted to the effect that some signallers were needed to make up the strength. So a pal and I went in for a course and passed.

Soon after we arrived in Malta the disaster of Messina[4] took place, and we distinctly felt the shock of the earthquake in Malta. All the beds on one side of the rooms in Floriana slid across to the other side of the room when she tilted us up one end. We went down on loading parties to load up some of our cruisers with flour and foodstuffs for the relief of the sufferers in Messina.

Another sight we were treated to was the burning of the Pilgrim Ship *SS Sardinia*[5] just at the mouth of the Grand Harbour. We could see them jumping from the burning decks into the sea. Bodies were being fished out for days after.

We are beginning to see the world. I went with a few more pals to Fort Manoor, which was to be the signaller's quarters, and after going through a course known as "the young hands course" I passed out with something to spare and became a full blown signaller. I was now entitled to my first badge on two years good conduct, and after going through my first course known as the "old hands course", I became entitled to wear the crossed flags above my GC badge. I'm now a fully trained signaller. [Aren't we getting on!]? Well peacetime soldiering is just "one darned thing after another", so the weeks, months and years roll around till we find ourselves getting real "old timers".

Kaiser Wilhelm II reviews the Somerset Light Infantry in Malta

We had a visit from King Edward in 1909 or 10, on his yacht the *Medina*, and, of course, we had a review parade and march past on the Malta racecourse out there. We also had a visit from "Kaiser Bill" during my stay in Malta, and if I knew then that he was going to give me such a "rough passage" in a few years hence, I think I should have clumped him one, as I was close enough to him to do it, as he drove through the narrow Maltese High Street, [Strada Reale]. However I did not clump him, so that's another story.

Still we are seeing the world and the "big people". I've seen the Kaiser and King Edward, I've seen the Prince of Wales [in France], the Duke of Connaught, but I've never yet seen King George, or Queen Mary, or Princess Mary, so I've just missed the best of the bunch. Still I'm living in hopes of seeing 'em all before I take the "long trail". So let's get back on the rails again.

Malta I would like to say, from my point of view, is about the best station in the world for troops, at least it was in my time; I cannot answer for what they do to 'em now out there. We had every kind of sport, both land and water, football, cricket, running, tug-o-war land and water, boat races, water polo, high diving, and swimming races. What more do you want than that blended with good food and shelter, good clothes, plenty of money, and heaps of time to spend it? That's the life boy! Of course we had our whack to do as regards training and "manoeuvres" and shooting and signalling courses, but taking it all around my three years soldiering in Malta was glorious, regardless of the fact that I was bitten by a snake of some sort on my left arm and was taken to hospital on Christmas morning, 1910. I was out on a signal station one day just before Christmas, and was lying flat on the ground reading a message through the telescope. It was an urgent message I remember, when suddenly I felt a stab on my bare arm and just caught a glimpse of a spotted tail sliding away in the grass at my side. I had to stick it until the message was finished, and when I looked at my arm it was all inflamed and swelling fast. As it was getting so near Christmas I did not "report sick", and, of course, it got worse daily till I could stick it no longer, and when I did report I was taken straight away in an ambulance wagon to hospital on Christmas morning. When the doctor saw it he made a fuss and said he had a mind to report me for not reporting sick earlier, and that I should be lucky if I did not lose my arm. I must be lucky, as I have still got it!

Going East

Well, as I said, the weeks, months, and years went around, and one day we had the news that we were off to China. Phew, now for seeing a bit of the old Globe, that was the news to give to troops! Although we were now seasoned troops we were like a lot of school kids as the prospect of a trip to the land of almond eyes and yellow skins. And one day we steamed out of the Grand Harbour, Malta, en route for the Far East on the good old tub *Somali*.

She was about the best old boat I've been on. Of course we had a right royal send-off from Malta, by the pals we were leaving behind, and also by the other regiments stationed there, bands playing, flags flying, and all that sort of thing, not forgetting a few heartbroken Maltese girls, who may or may not have healed them with another regiment after we left. I, myself,

The Somersets on board the Somali

left a nice bit of "Maltese lace" behind, as did most of our chaps [bless 'em].

We got to Port Said in about 3 or 4 days, and on down and through the Suez Canal, and through the Straits Settlements to Singapore. Then the old tub steps it out once more on her way up to Hong Kong, where we were taken ashore for another leg stretcher and once more we got away on the last lap away up north to a place called Chingwangtao, where we arrived about October 26th 1911 after being bumped aboard by several different types of weather since September 12th.

Well now I have briefly given you a glimpse of our run from Malta to Chingwangtao. Later on I'll try to describe the sights en route, but while I think of it I would like to mention this. On the trip out I volunteered to do "standing guard" which meant that a few more pals and I would be on guard every third night and were not to be taken for any more duties in between. One night as we were nearing Hong Kong from Singapore I was on sentry down between the decks in the married quarter berths. It was a hot sultry night and little wind going, but a heavy under swell was making the old *Somali* roll a bit. Of course being a hot night all the portholes were open and the "wind scoops" were out to catch what wind was going. The boat gave an extra big roll during the night watch and I heard a woman's scream, and a sudden rush of water. I dashed down to the berth where I could see the water coming from, oh dear, how can I describe it; anyway there was a young married woman and a little kiddie sitting in about a foot of seawater in their night dresses and all the bunks were simply drowned out. I rescued a lot of underwear, shirts and stockings etc, etc, [and other things that I cannot spell], and closed the porthole after pulling in the wind scoop. The wind scoop had done a bit of overtime and had scooped up a few gallons of sea as well as wind. It was exciting while it lasted and it was looked on as all in a day's work, or rather a night's work.

China Station

Well now, we are at Chingwangtao, so we disembarked and loaded all the baggage on a train for Tientsin.

After about eighteen months up there I found myself "in orders" for

Trooping the Colour in Tientsin

England. At the time we were encamped in the Gobi Desert, North China, Doubtless you know that during 1911 and 1912 the revolution of China was going on. Well of course we were "under orders" for anything for months. It was the same kind of thing in a smaller scale to what is taking place out there at present, but I'll tell you later of some of the jobs we had in hand at that time. But in passing, I would say that I have a cutting taken from the *Bath Herald* of 1912 and sent out to me in China recordings the doings of a "gallant band of Somersets"[6]. That was when the Major of one of the companies of Somersets told the Chinese mob that they would only pass over the dead bodies of his men. Well that's a brief outline of soldiering abroad, and as I said just now while we were in the Gobi Desert I was informed that I was one of the draft which would be coming home to England the following winter. I have a distinct recollection of marching into the Commanding Officer's Marquee pitched in the desert on a cold wet miserable morning, and of marching out again with my discharge papers marked, "Exemplary, Sober, Intelligent, Reliable and a hard working man" [evidently the old man's bacon was cooked well that morning]. But putting jokes on one side, Col Everett was as fine a Colonel as any "Tommy" could wish for. Well now in due course the day came round when those of us who were bound for "Blighty" had to say good-bye to the old pals, and get aboard a train for Chingwangtao once again.

Return to 'Blighty'

We eventually arrived there and found the old transport *Soudan* waiting for us. Getting aboard her was easy, and we steamed away for Hong Kong as the first stop, where we stayed for eight days, and then found the *Soudan* had to go on around Africa via the Cape, so we were shipped to the old *Rohilla* once more. Well, to make a long story short we arrived at

Southampton on the 21st December, and went to Gosport by an "accident", but really I think it was more by design on the part of a certain Colour-Sergeant who shall be nameless, and who thought that by sending me to Gosport discharge depot instead of going with him to the 1st Battalion at Borden he would get out of having to pay back the £1 he borrowed to go ashore at Columbo. However we met at the Borden Camp [Alton], where I went after spending two days at Gosport. From Borden Camp I came to Bath for two months leave, arriving at the GWR Bath Station at 8pm on Christmas Eve 1912, just in time for Christmas 'eh. Well after my two months leave was up I went back to Borden to finish my time and after a few months in Blighty [England] soldiering in Major Prowse's Company at Borden I was finally transferred to the Army Reserve Section A in October 1913. Of course I had what is known as a "working furlough" and left Borden in August 1913. I spent the next two months looking for work. Now, if you excuse my rubbing it in, I would just like to repeat that my character was marked Exemplary, with Sober, Intelligent, Reliable and Hard working man tacked on. Also I was in possession of a 3rd class educational certificate, had I wished I could have sat for my 2nd class one, and doubtless got it. I also had a Mounted Infantry certificate and I had earned it, as we used to ride and break in our own Mongolian ponies out in China. I was a thoroughly trained signaller, I was also a marksman at shooting, and I was in splendid condition physically.

CHAPTER 2

Life as a 'Civvy' 1913–14

Now I have not told you all that, reader, just for the sake of boasting, but for a reason, which I'll soon show you. I came away from the Army in 1913 proud of my record, and I'm still proud of it, and would gladly go back again if I could, not because I'm such a patriotic "bloke" there's no holding me back when bullets are flying about thickest, oh dear no, but because we were paid, fed, housed, and clothed in a manner which made one feel that he was a human being and not a savage, or, even an animal, as the conditions of work in civil life made one feel just before the war, [they're not much better today by the way]. If I had my time over again I would most certainly have been a twenty one years man, and my advice to all young 'uns of 18 or 19 years of age is to enlist in a good old county regiment and see the world for free, not let the blood-sucking employers of labour drain your life's blood away for a coolies wage, whilst they ride to their big dinners with a big fat cigar stuck in their "gills"; and maybe when they have drained it they will give you your tram fare to the workhouse, or maybe again they won't. However I maintain that any man coming home from "furrin parts" with a character like that shouldn't have much trouble in landing a job, also I reckon by way of a joke, that when a troopship is coming thro' the Bay with a man aboard with a character like that [not forgetting the trimmings], the skipper of the said troopship should give orders for "sparks" to call up "all stations" and let the glad news be broadcasted to enable the employers of these returning soldiers and sailors from "furrin parts", to go to the dock side at Southampton to greet the said man with open arms and say unto him, "I'll give you a job, £3 per week [perhaps], all found etc. etc. "Thank you very much and all that". But no, character or no character, I found that a man had to do his own "scrounging" for a job, so after I was finally transferred to the Reserve, I got on the "scrounge" for a job, and this is my experience. Mind you reader, I'm talking now of October 1913.

I think I'll call it "the diary of a Civvy Ex-soldier", or perhaps, "Looking for work and finding it" would be more suitable. However after a prolonged struggle with several thousand other would be assassins of labour I managed to get a job at the Bath Gas Works. The wage was 10/- per week, with as much small coal as one could comfortably eat. I was put on several different kinds of jobs in about a month or 6 weeks, and, I believe, I earned the reputation of making a good fist at all of them. One I remember consisted of digging a trench down through a wooded garden to lay pipes, at Simpley Stokeways. Another consisted of climbing a mountain of coke to keep the hole clear where the coke fell through. I was game for anything [and I'm still of the same mind]. Was I not marked on my discharge papers as a "Hard-working man", and was I not getting the magnificent sum of 19/- per week? I ask you. But the "tin hat" was put on my enthusiasm one day when the yard foreman, Mr Bodman, came to me and said "Here me son, I've got a little job for you to do. Just go in there and ask for a Mr Chambers and he will show you what he wants done". Now me being a good soldier bubbling over with discipline, I said, "right ho", and went in to pay Mr Chambers a call. I found him, and I also found about half a dozen railway trucks loaded with small coal drawn up in front of some furnaces. Mr C handed me a shovel with his compliments and these words; "These trucks have got to be unloaded and the quicker it is done the better it will be for you [or him]". I forget which, but I've an idea now that it was good for him, as he had the job piecework and I was on day work. Draw your own conclusions. But me being an "innocent soldier" just returned to "civvy life", I did not tumble to it quite so readily as I should if it happened today. We live and we learn. However, seeing that I was a "hard working man" [according to my discharge papers], it did not take me long to knock a big dent in that contract, and Mr Chambers was evidently so pleased with himself and me that when I unloaded that lot he had the empty trucks shunted out and another string of full ones shunted in. I guess he thought I'd be bored doing nothing. Anyhow I played "Put and Take" with trucks of small coal for a couple of days till it suddenly dawned on me that I was getting in a terrible mess by "knocking off" time daily. These trucks, I may repeat, were unloaded in front of the furnaces which threw out a lot of heat as hot as the place the "Padre" used to speak of at church on Sundays. The coal was small and very dusty, and I was a "hard working man", don't I forget, consequently I used to sweat streams, and small coal dust sweat being of a very loveable disposition towards each other, I leave you to guess what I used to look like each evening about 5pm. No miner was ever blacker than yours truly, and all for 19/- per week. I ask you. Well it struck me one day that I should be far better off in a home as it were. So I politely informed the great Mr C. that I had an ample sufficiency of throwing small coal about. He replied, as near as I can remember "Thee's have to do it". I answered in words to this effect "show me anybody in these darn works that would make me do it", and I promptly flung the shovel at him and jumped out of the coal truck. I made my way to Mr Bodman, the yard foreman who had sent me on the job. His greeting was "What's up son"? So I explained the situation to him, and his advice was to go back and get on with it. Now I would not accept that advice. I said that I'd sooner pack it up. So as he had no other job he could find me just then, in due course I found myself "on 'the carpet", facing the manager, [I nearly said Colonel]. How I trembled, I don't think, although as my character shows, I was not in the habit of "being for the high jump" as we called it in the service. Well now the manager [Mr Ellery I think his name was] was a very nice old gent, and he asked my trouble, and once again I explained. I received the same fatherly advice viz – go to it, but remembering the motto on the RE cap badge [Honi soi qui mal y pense], I politely refused, at the same time pointing out to him that the money that was handed out to me on pay day, although very clean itself, was not enough to enable me to buy a sufficient amount of soap to clean myself to handle it. The old gentleman, crestfallen at my outburst, and his aide-de-camp [a Mr Gardner at that time], who was also present at the "court-martial" over my revolutionary activities, looked at me aghast. And if this little narrative is ever allowed in print and should catch his eye, maybe he will recall it, if his memory serves as well as mine does. Well after a little palaver amongst themselves, while I stood wondering if I would be shot at dawn, or just simply hung, the manager turned and spoke to me, "We have decided, on account of the splendid character that you hold, to overlook this and to give you another chance, etc etc". He was willing to overlook the fact that I had pointed out a few home truths, and was wanting me to go back and consume some more small coal. Ye gods, I thought at the time that that was one disadvantage of holding a good character. Anyhow I did not see eye to eye with that arrangement, and so the makers of coke and your 'umble servant dissolved partnership. And to get a job like that I believe I had to pass a doctor, when I had only just left the service absolutely physically fit, in splendid condition, marksman, trained signaller etc.etc, three bags full. Well now that's job number one on my adventure in "civvy life".

Here's another. About this time men were wanted for the work of temporary postmen during the Christmas rush 1913, so on making a few enquires at the East Twerton post office as to particulars, I was informed by Miss Hayes, as she then was, who knew me personally, that they were full up but to go to the GPO, ask for Mr Salter, say she sent me, and all would be well. I followed her instructions, and lo and behold, it was so. Mr Salter kindly glanced at my army papers, and as a man of brains would do, put me on straight away. Within an hour of meeting Mr Salter I was up on the Landsdown's "giddy heights" clearing letterboxes. I was also retained for the New Year push, and for about a week or more. I spent a very enjoyable Christmas 1913 walking around Bath with other people's "puddens and pies", etc. In the whole of that time I was only offered one drink, and that was by a good lady in some little house along Whiteway Road, Tiverton Hill. She offered me a glass of port wine as I handed her a registered letter on Christmas Day about dinnertime. I politely refused it, [had I not had "Sober" marked on my character?] As regards my connection with the Post Office, I would like to mention in passing that when I was "a serving of His Majesty" out in China I was asked with others what employment I desired on my return to "civvy life". I registered as Postman, Tram-driver, or Porter, and I believe from "information received" [as they say in Police talk], that a pal of mine Tom Todd [killed in action], was first for postman, and your 'umble was second when the war broke out and claimed us both. Poor old Tommy's life story ended at "Mons", mine is being related here, such as it is.

Now all good things good or bad, come to an end, as the bird said when he swallowed a foot long worm, so did my job as temporary postman do likewise much to my regret, and once more I find myself cooling my heels in the snow of Jan 1914, if there was any. Walking in town one day I met a pal who considered I'd soon get a job on the railway if I cared to. Well I did care to, and although for the moment I forget the procedure I took, suffice it to say, that after a rigmarole of passing doctors, sight tests, and reading of characters [I almost said palms], I landed a job on the MR. It consisted of walking around the Avonmouth docks with tarpaulin sheets on one's head covering up any loaded truck that was ready to go on it's journey. Another 19/- per week job. I went to Avonmouth to fix up some "diggings", and I was offered some at Richmond Terrace at 16/- per week, which I at first took, but, on coming back to Bath, as I had to start work the following Monday, I met another pal, and told him I'd got a job at Avonmouth sheeting trucks, and I had just been down to fix up "digs". I gave him the address and price per week, but he gave me an address where he used to "dig" in Napier Road, and told me to go there on the Monday morning with my kit and mention him. I did so, and found I'd struck the nicest little shanty in Avonmouth. A very nice old couple, the old man [Jimmy Duffett by name], being one of the old sea dogs who sailed the seas before I was hatched, and him and I had many a laughable argument as to what Malta was like in his time and what it was like when I was out there. The old cock used to swear there was no soil there for "growing spuds", but when I used to say we had a racecourse out there and grass football pitches etc, he would rave and say I'd never been there or else, or else I must have got the place mixed up with the Isle of Wight, [laugh, by crumbs]. Anyhow Richmond Terrace did not see me as the old folks fixed me up for 10/- per week excluding weekends, or 12/- inclusive, which was better than 16/- inclusive at Richmond Terrace. Besides I had an idea that after I paid 16/- each week for "digs", I should not be left with an over flush of cash for charity and train fares for Bath occasionally working on a 19/- per week job.

On the way down with my kit on the Monday morning I was given a good opportunity of seeing what some people will do when they think there is some money lying about spare. This is how it came about. I had all my best clothes on with about 5 hundredweight [more or less] of spare kit in a big dress basket and as the train ran into Clifton Down Station, where I had to change for the 'Mouth, I tried to heave my basket out of the carriage but got it jammed in the door. Mind you it was a good hefty lump of kit I had in those days, and I supposed I looked as if I was going abroad again or something, seeing as I was all dressed up as it were. Anyhow, the guard of the train seeing me wrestling with this darned basket, nipped across the platform and with much bowing and scraping he got me free and asked me "where to sir?" I replied with a twang "I guess I'm hitting the trail for "little old Avonmouth, Bo". Now we had a regiment of Americans stationed up in Tientsin quite near us and as our fellows and the Yanks used to mix fairly freely, perhaps I had caught the twang for the time being [perhaps I say], as I had often heard the Yankee troops make use of the expression "that they were hitting trails". Anyway I said it natural enough to deceive the guard, who must have got the impression that I was some "Golden Guy of a Yank" on my way to Kentucky or Oklahoma overflowing with dollar bills, as he took my basket on his shoulder and carried it along the platform to where he said the train would pull in for the 'Mouth" in 15 minutes, putting it nicely on the seat with the remark "There you are sir"[Sir, mind on 19/- per week]. I thanked him very much in my best Yankee twang, just to keep up the deception, and hoped it kept fine for him etc, and then pulled out a packet of "gaspers" [Woodbines, 5 a penny, all made to stand up], and offered him one, and lit up one for myself. Honestly speaking everybody, I believe that guard would have liked to flatten me [if he dared] and also he had a mind to hand in his resignation letter there and then. How was he to know I was only a truck sheeter on the huge wage of 19/- per week, I ask you? Still it goes to show what some people will do when they think there is something on the end of it, and there's no harm in a good think.

Well, let's get back to the rails again. The weeks rolled by, and I used to run up to Bath for the weekend sometimes, and on one of my raids on Bath I met a man [now dead] who was a foremen of a big works there. Now he thought he could get me a start where he was at 19/- [that perpetual 19/-, it haunts me yet]. By the way, I don't think some people had learnt to reckon up to 20 just before the war, as they were always saying 19 anyhow. However I thought 19/- in Bath would be more profitable than 19/- at the 'Mouth with train fare to pull out, so I told him to go ahead and get me a job, which he did. I was sorry indeed to leave the old diggings down in Avonmouth, as I had enjoyed every minute of my stay down there, and it was grand to see the Royal George and Royal Edward arriving there and departing to and from Canada, or the Patuca, Bayano, and others coming home from Kingston, Jamaica loaded with bananas. Still I've learnt that to live even in those times, owing to the high rate of wages paid, one must go to where the bread is cut thickest, so I say goodbye to Avonmouth [job number 3] and come to Bath to start on job number 4. This is March 1914.

The same old procedure having been gone through, such as an argument with the Labour Exchange, doctors inspection, reading of character, etc.etc, I was engaged to help some! [Now let's make sure of my footing here as I am still working there]. Anyhow this firm I refer to now is a big one, and sends work all over the globe, as I have loaded plenty for shipment to "furrin parts", so I'll just say that I was put with a few more men and told to make myself useful, and as time wore on I was handed a funny looking machine and was told that with luck it would bore holes in anything. Well I had a go at it and my luck must have been in with this thing, as I certainly did drill some holes. They were not exactly where the fellow wanted them but that did not cause me any grey hairs. It was the same old thing done day after day and I was getting more proficient at this hole making business, and the days and weeks flew by till we find ourselves into July 1914. Now readers you know without me telling you that the war clouds were gathering about this time, and I knew it well enough as I was on the Army Reserve. Also I know that the particular people I was working for just before the Great War have a nasty habit of giving their employees a week's holiday in August [without pay]. A holiday is needful and useful, provided you are prepared for it. But if one happened to be married with two or three kiddies and a wife to provide for, on the princely sum of 19/-per week, how in God's name can these employers expect them to be prepared for a holiday of a week's duration. It's all very well for the £5, £6, £7 and £10 per week man, who had to pay no more for his bread, butter, milk, eggs, coal etc.etc, than the 19/- man. He can well afford to take this week, or even a months holiday, to play cricket, tennis, and go boating etc. Oh yes, I know you may wish to say to yourself that I'm jealous of them earning it, but I'm not the slightest degree jealous of anyone who can earn money. Good luck to them, but I do think it would be much more human to the "underdog" to let him go into work after a couple of days holiday if he wished to. I could name men who have not recovered financially from August, before Christmas is upon them, and then they have the same old trouble all over again. So, after getting that lot off my chest I'll get on with the story.

Well, as I said before, the war clouds are gathering and we are just now, in fancy, at the beginning of August 1914.

CHAPTER 3

War: August 1914

The firm I was working for shut down for the usual weeks "lock-out", and August Bank Holiday Tuesday I took a trip to Bournemouth for the day, and while there I heard war had been declared. On returning to Bath I saw a notice posted on the wall of the Drill Hill, Lower Bristol Road, warning all Army Reservists to join their regiments without delay. The next day Wednesday, a few old pals and myself off Reserve took the train from Bath for Taunton, our Depot town. I have no recollection of getting a ticket or railway warrant or anything else, only I know we pushed off in a hurry and no one stopped us. Well, we arrived at the Depot and it was the "reunion of souls". By crumbs, some of my old pals had not done any work since we came home from China, and were in rags. Others had put their very oldest clothes on and were nearly as bad. But although, and mark this well, these old pals were in rags, some "down and out" and broke, we were pals and were all soon sharing out our different parcels which we had brought with us. As "civvies" you cannot understand what it was like when the "Old Contemptible" were together. That's where you find real chums, in the Service. Well we hung about waiting to get our khaki, rifles and equipment "dished out" to us, which was being done as fast as a dozen or more "old sweats" [old soldiers] could do it. Mind you the Depot was choked right full with reservists from Sections A, B and D. We got our khaki and straps by next day, so we had the luck to sleep there one night. We were packed into the rooms about 100 strong, which normally held about 30 or 40. The same day as our little dozen arrived, they were packing them off in batches of 30 down to the station and off to Colchester, but for some reason or other we were kept till the afternoon of Thursday till we were about 500 strong, and then formed up headed by the Depot band. We marched off to the station to the tune of – no, not Tipperary – but the "Boys of the Old Brigade".

]PS Please excuse me writing in "Tommy" language, but as I write I am living it all over again. Thank you.[

If I live to be 500 years old I'll never forget that march through the packed, decorated streets of Taunton. How these people cheered us, because you see, although the lads were in some cases in rags the day before, when we got the khaki on once again, and the old "bond hook" [rifle] on our soldiers once more, and the feel of the "harness" around our bodies, and swinging along behind the band just like old times, we just couldn't help pulling our shoulders back and chins in, and the band simply had to play that stirring tune "The Boys of the Old Brigade", as that was just what we were. Nearly 500 strong of the "Old Contemptible" off to the "Front", flags, handkerchiefs, sunshades, umbrellas, hats and all sorts waving and flying in the air; mothers, sisters, wives and sweethearts crying and laughing in turns. Oh, it was great, that march to Taunton Station and after a struggle, we arrived and entrained for Colchester, being there about a week to get "squared up" a bit, and then moved to Harrow. We were about a week there doing marches and learning the way to bandage yourself to prevent bleeding to death, when Fritz hits your head off with a shell. [How cheerful.]

Then one day we packed up all of a sudden and entrained. We knew not where for until we got there, and found ourselves in Southampton. Then we knew "summat". We embarked and slid quietly out of the harbour in the evening and slipped across the channel to Le Havre where we arrived on Sunday 22nd August at dawn.

France

We could hear cries of "Vive les Anglais" and "Heep, Heep, Hurrah" being yelled to us by the Frenchies as we drew nearer the quay in the grey mist of the dawn, and having made fast to the quay wall we straightaway disembarked on to the soil of France. I've often thought of how many lads stepped ashore on to French soil never to leave it again. Once ashore we formed up and marched up a long hill to a camp somewhere on the hills behind Havre, which had been prepared for us, and had a breakfast. We stayed in that camp until the evening of the 22nd August and were visited by all the French mademoiselles of Havre who gave us fruits of all

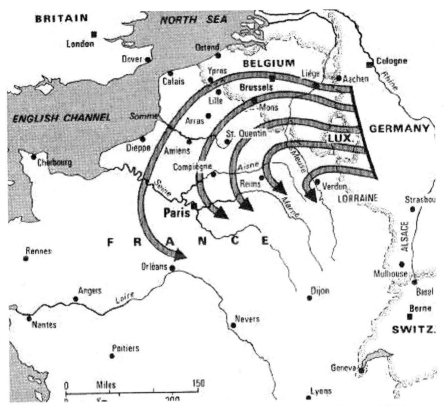

The Von Schlieffen Plan – Germany's planned attack on France 1914

description, and flowers and wine, so in return we gave them our cap badges and the brasses from the shoulder straps till it was rather difficult to tell what regiment anyone belonged to. I might mention that when our 500 reservists arrived at Colchester we joined up with the regiment there, so of course by then, we were the 1st Battalion of the "Prince Albert's Somersetshire Light Infantry, and as "good a mob" as ever went "over there". Still that's another story.

Into Action

Well, on the evening on the 22nd August we came down the hill again and entrained in a French train. By crumbs, what a difference from ours! Of course we had another send off by the French people from Havre. I suppose they knew we were "for it" somewhere up the line, and wanted

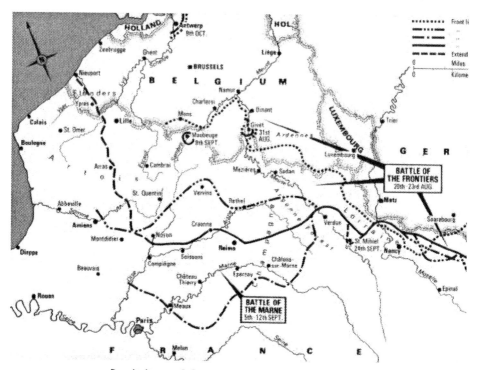

Battle lines of Germany's attack on France 1914

Timescale of the early part of the war on the Western Front	
August 4th	Britain declares war on Germany
August 13th	BEF lands and moves into Belgium
August 23rd and 24th	The battle of Mons
August 26th	The battle of Le Cateau
September 7th to 10th	The battle of the Marne
September 12th to 15th	The battle of the Aisne
October 10th to November 2nd	The battle of Le Bassee
October 12th to November 2nd	The battle of Messines
October 13th to November 2nd	The battle of Armentières
October 19th to November 22nd	The 1st battle of Ypres

to make our last few days on earth as happy as possible for us. Sob stuff [wait a minute reader while I get my hanky out]. Not only that, were we not come across to fight for France and kill all the Fritzs in about 10 minutes? Rough stuff [wait a minute reader while I load my rifle]. Anyhow, after crawling all over the north of France looking for a place to stop the train, the driver at last decided to stop at Le Cateau [I suppose the poor devil was only obeying orders though]. So we stopped at Le Cateau and got out. We didn't pay the engine driver 'cos we never had any money. Still we wandered about the countryside for a couple of days, and I remember a railway station named "Solesmes"[7] where I was put near a round water tower on "lookout". My first sight of a German in the Great War was an officer prisoner, the charge of about a dozen French Tommies. Why he had a dozen to look after him I don't know, unless he was someone very important and they didn't want to lose him.

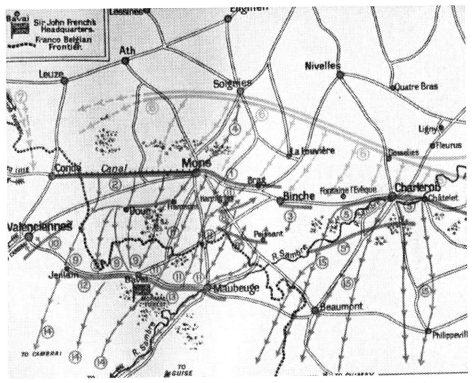

Scene of the chief operations near Mons and Charleroi – August 1914

CHAPTER **4**

The Retreat from Mons and the Action at Le Cateau

It was getting dusk I well remember, as I could see the flashes of the guns and shells bursting just ahead of us where some sort of scrap was going on. We were now waiting for our chance to swipe old "Fritz" one, and had been served out with bully and biscuits and our "iron rations", which was our "last hope" in the event of getting no more from anywhere else. We had sudden orders just before it got very dark to form up on a field there and move back. We had no idea what was on the go or where we were, and I don't believe that the "brass hats" really knew what they were doing. Well we did not go into action that night but kept on the move somewhere. Sleep and food was a thing which did not seem to be on the programme at all. We used to drink water from the wells of the houses, eat fruit from the garden, beg bread and biscuits when we could, which was very seldom, believe me.

Well now, to make a long story short, on the eve of the 26th August 1914 we were near a little village called Ligny not far from Mons[8], and I well remember that we were just turned out hurriedly from a barn, which our little platoon had occupied for the night. We had just made some tea, bagged some bread and fat cooked bacon from somewhere when the order came to "stand to" ready to go up over a sloping field "into action" to meet our old pal Fritz. I don't expect any of the lads who came out of that scrap alive will ever forget going up that long slope at Ligny without a bit of cover, and the bullets whistling past our heads. Remember reader, the "Old Contemptibles" had no steel helmets to stop bullets when we went out and I remember turning up the collar of my khaki tunic and pulling my hat well down to keep the bullets out. "Wind up". Of course I had the "wind up", who there didn't? But we still went up to the top unless we were killed en route. The only cover we had was the stacks of wheat, which were piled up in the fields by the farmers who had fled leaving their crops. Just try to picture the long lines of troops going up into action, every nerve braced up, every eye flashing fire and every heart beating quicker, believe me. There we go, a long steady line about three paces apart and just as we had done on manoeuvres on Salisbury Plain. There was no panic, no hurry. They were as steady as a rock. One would cough and fall dead here maybe, another would give a yelp and drop over there, but the rest of us went slowly but surely up that terrible field till we neared the top. As we drew nearer the bullets came thicker and faster and the lads began to drop dead faster and thicker to. God it was awful to be going up that field never knowing any second when one of those damned spiteful machine gun bullets would get you in the head and hurl you to the next world. [We are in action near Mons.]

When we did get to the top of the slope we found a bit of a country road running along the top of it straight across our front and a bit of a bank at the side of it. I see it all now as clearly as it was only this morning. I reckon it was about 11am or noon when we finally got up there. The sun was high I well remember as it made the human blood smell horrible. Just about 20 yards to the right of where I flung myself on the bank to open fire, was a little bit of a copse about 30 yards square with a shrine in it facing the road. Now the battle was on in earnest and the noise was deafening, bombs, rifle fire, machine guns in heaps and shrapnel were bursting all over us. We could see the Fritzs down over the slope blazing away at us, and we fired like hell till our rifles grew hot. I hear the cry of the band boy now crying for his mother as he had lost his food. I see now the fellow lying next to me on my left getting a bullet smack in the head and dying without a sound. But it drove his nose into the bank as though someone had used a big hammer on the back of his head. I saw a certain sergeant take his wife's photo from his pocket and kiss it goodbye. I still see a pal leap in the air clutching his throat with the blood gushing through his fingers like a fountain. Reader, words fail me to describe all I saw when I first went into action in the Great War. We lay there firing and firing with bullets tearing up the ground and throwing dirt in our faces. It seemed to me that we were doing awful slaughter over there but my gods our lads were dying fast too. Our fire seemed to be slackening and it was constantly being yelled at us "Keep on firing" or "Don't slacken the fire" or "Blaze away", but reader, I ask you "How can dead men shoot"? Suddenly we

heard yells and shouts behind us and when I turned to look I saw a
sergeant pointing towards some ruined houses a little way down the road
to the right. We could not see what he could see from our positions as the
little copse which I had spoken of just now stopped our view, but it
appears that the troops on the right have been forced to retire and Fritz
was attacking us on the flank as well as in front, and let me tell you this a
minute; when a line of troops are firing like hell and machine guns are
spitting 'em out, those shouts have to be very loud and long to be heard
even a few yards away, so that by the time we did hear them Fritz was
coming along in line about 300 yards away. We were told to drop back
and face right and "let them have it". As I ran across bent double to take
my share I caught a glimpse of old Major Prowse[9] lying there with the sun
glittering on his bald head. He was lying amongst a patch of sugar beet,
encouraging the lads and directing the fire just as if on manoeuvres at
home. When we had the order to drop back and face right I was amazed
to see how few of my old pals complied with the order. I thought they had
not heard it, as only about 20 or 30 rushed across to blaze at Fritz again.
Reader, the reason was not through disobedience, but simply the fact that
those lads were either dead or too badly wounded to move. Just think,
reader, only a few short hours before we were a merry little band of pals,
making tea together in the early morn, and stealing pears out of the
orchards around us, and now they would never want any more tea or
pears. That's war reader. I often wonder how many mothers, wives, sisters
and sweethearts know just how their lads died out there. If the womenfolk
only knew there would never be any more war throughout the world, as
I'm sure they would not breed sons to be slaughtered in that way.
However let's get on.

Things by now were beginning to look desperate for our little band, as we
were getting it at the front and flank and when those of us who dropped
back started to shoot we had given up the only bit of cover we had, and
had to lay out in the open. I can still hear those bullets plunging into the
ground, and I can still hear those coughs and grunts when a pal stopped a
bullet and started off on his last, long, journey. We fired as mad as ever we
could to stop Fritz from coming ahead and could see his troops dropping
in bunches, which must have had the effect of halting them, as they
suddenly stopped advancing and lay out blazing away at us all the more. I
never expected to see another sunrise. Things now seemed to have come
to a standstill, and Fritz would not come on, and we daren't go back so we

lay there sniping at each other for some time, when I heard someone yell out "How bist off for 'ammo up there kid?" That made me search my pouches, and 'twas then I discovered I had not a round in them. I opened the breech of my gun and found I had 4 or 5 rounds only. When we went up that slope in the morning we each had 150 rounds of ammunition on us, so you can guess how we had been "blazing" 'em into Fritz's advancing troops, and what's more we didn't have to take "careful aim" at them. It was just like firing into the hedge of a field, only it was a human being hedge. I remember hearing during the war that the Kaiser was supposed to have said that every British Tommy was issued with a machine gun at Mons, but I reckon it was the "Old Contemptibles" [15 rounds per minute] that he was thinking about. Bad as our predicament was I would not have changed places with Fritz for something as it must have been murderous for them advancing into our fire. When we discovered how short of ammunition we were we yelled for more and I saw an arm swing up out of the patch of sugar beet in which we were lying now, and a web-sling of "ammo" came flying towards me [50 rounds] followed by another and another. We soon grabbed these and passed them along the line. I was glad, believe me, as I remember thinking, now if old Fritz charges we shall give him the last few rounds and nip to it, or shall I keep the last round for myself like they told us in the Chinese revolutions. But when I handled this other 50 rounds I felt braver, only I didn't tell Fritz so. Fritz had stopped advancing by now, and had quietened down a little, perhaps on account of our fire, or maybe, shortage of ammo. All the time this had been going on the stretcher bearers were working like slaves to get the badly wounded ones away but they had a thankless task as they were getting shot down themselves.

We suddenly received orders to drop back down the slope in twos and threes to the railway track at the bottom of the hill behind us. Those who were not actually retiring had to keep firing at Fritz to make him stop his firing. But of course you may guess what with the killed, wounded and some retiring we could not hope to stop all the Fritzs from firing, so as soon as any of us got up on one knee to start the long dash down the hill we were promptly fired at. Those who were very badly wounded had to be left there to be taken prisoner, as it was simply impossible to get them away, and it was more human and a little safer for them to be flat on the ground than to be carried away slowly and be killed en route, as once we had left the ground we simply had to run like hares for the railway bank.

When it came to my turn I raised myself off the ground with one arm to see who was going to run with me [as we were all spread out 5 or 10 yards apart now to make it look like there were more of us, and with the dead pals lying between us], and I saw a pal named Tim Rowsell lying about 10 yards down the hill on my right [I heard he was drowned in the mud of the "Plug Street" trench later on in the War when it collapsed on them]. I yelled "Ready Tim", he said "OK" and we jumped and sped away down the hill like racehorses; old Tim Rowsell had a few yards start on me but I soon caught him up and passed him, and I reckon we were both doing a mile a minute, more or less, when old Tim went down smack rolling over and over like a shot rabbit. I might say here that as soon as each two or three of us got up to dash back, Fritz would normally fire from the ruined houses at us with a machine gun he had fixed up there. Well I pulled up and turned back to old Tim and asked him if he had got it, as I thought a bullet surely must have got him. He stopped rolling now and was lying flat puffing like a sea-pig, really it was more like a rhinoceros, only I cannot spell it, so I called it as sea-pig. He was too puffed to speak, so I said again "Where bist hit"? then he gasped out "I dunno", so after feeling himself all over to see where he was hit, and finding nothing wrong, I said "stand up, and see where the pain is" [forgetting old Fritz and his machine gun for a minute]. Now I've seen some quick movements done out in France, and as soon as Tim stood up [to see if he was dead or not], old Fritz let go at him with that dammed gun. Tim bobbed down, grabbed his gun, up again and was off like a blinking aeroplane before I could move. Of course I did not sit there viewing the scenery, as I was not in love with the locality, so I scooted after Tim, and all that little lot was caused by Tim's puttee coming unwound from his leg and tripping him up as he ran. Thus as far as Tim Rowsell and your 'umble self was concerned the "Retreat from Mons" commenced.

Well, we arrived at the railway embankment at the bottom of the hill, and at once took up the position to cover the retreat of others coming down. There were not many, I'm sorry to say, and I saw a few more lads throw up their arms and pitch headlong, during that mad dash down the hill. While we were actually on the railway track we were safe from rifle and machine gun fire, as Fritz could not see us, and I was glad to see old Major Prowse jogging down the hill still with his hat in his hand. When he reached us he decided the railway was not a very nice place to hold on account of the rising ground behind us, up which we would have to go later, and it would be safer to go up now that we had stopped Fritz for a bit, than it would be to wait till he came down the slope and peppered us going up. Because, you see, we had lost so many men up there and Fritz was coming on in thousands as soon as he had got his reinforcements up. At the top of the hill behind us was where we made our early morning breakfast. Fritz's guns were now shelling that village, and the Major told us to go back up the hill and rally near it before Fritz got on the move against the little village we had come down from in the early morning. So we moved back up the hill in extended order and as we mounted higher and higher Fritz gave us a bit of rifle fire to help us along, but as the range was pretty long we did not worry, after what we had been through up the other hill. But as we climbed that slope towards the village I heard all sorts of remarks as to how different pals had met their deaths. Three officers out of five had gone west, and no one seemed to know what company he was with, or who was in charge or anything else. We were hungry, thirsty, tired as dogs, sick with the smell of blood and the sights we had seen during the day, and by the time we arrived near the village it was nearly dusk. The Major caught up with us near the village and rallied about 30 of us into a little orchard on the outskirts and told us to dig some head cover for ourselves, as we should probably hold the village when old Fritz came on again. He went off to find out what orders he could get as to future movements.

I would just like to pay tribute here to some of those heroic French nuns which I saw near the village, bringing out sheets, pillows and blankets for our badly wounded lads saturated with blood. They gave us some wine and that which I tasted was the best drink I've ever had in my life I'll swear. Fritz was dropping big shells flop into the village near a monastery too, where these nuns were bringing out things. Well we started digging some head cover as ordered with our entrenching tools, but as we were only a little gang of about 30 strong, and did not have even a lance-corporal in charge of us now that the Major had left us, we did not dig very much before someone said "What's the good of doing this, as soon as we've got it done we shall have to move off somewhere else", someone else agreed and so that's how the job of digging did not get finished. So we started having a "scrounge" round the houses for some grub, as we had not eaten anything since that early morning meal in this same village, and now it was evening. During the course of a scrounge somebody found a sort of baker's shop from which the civvies had fled during the day leaving everything as it stood. Out in the yard were some fowls and rabbits waiting to be adopted [so we adopted them]. We got hold of a round brass kettle about 4 feet in circumference and 2 feet deep that had been used for boiling things in [perhaps dirty clothes for all we knew or cared]. About 8 or 10 fowls and two or three rabbits were soon "murdered" and cut up with our jack knives. Dressers and shutters up at the windows supplied the fire, and we soon had some sort of stew on the go. We had no luck as regards finding any bread though, although it was a baker's shop and we were in the bake house. Still with these fowls, rabbits, some spuds, and carrots and a few more odds and ends from our haversacks we made an Irish stew in a French bake house. Such items as flavouring didn't worry us, so after one of the funniest tasting meals I ever hope to have, we got down to it for a snooze, taking it for granted that the war was over for the night. [That's where Fritz gave us a shock.]

There were about 30 of us all bundled in this little bake house bent on having a sleep. We had a few fags between us, and some had dropped off to sleep and others were sitting up smoking. We had taken our straps off and put our rifles handy, but had not taken off boots or putties. Suddenly we heard a clatter of hoofs on the cobblestones outside. Someone grabbed a gun and went to the door to see what the row was about, and a voice in the darkness outside said, "Who's in charge in there?" He got the answer "All of us". "Well" he said, "all of us had better get out of it as quick as we could move, as Fritz is coming in at the other end of the village". Then there was a scramble. It was a cavalry patrol of ours who were keeping in touch with Fritz who had warned us to clear out quick. We dived for our guns and straps in the dark, and in about two minutes we were out on the road tracking in the direction the cavalry patrol had taken. We heard some rifle fire going on around us, but did not stop to ask Fritz the direction, believe me. Now as we had just gone through a day of Hell's treatment, and also had just got as comfortable as possible for the night, as we fondly imagined, to get turned out into the road about midnight to get a move on was not much to our liking, so, of course, there was heaps of grousing and cussing going on. In fact the air was blue, and, of course, as we had no officer now or even an NCO to control us [as we had not seen Major Prowse since he left us overnight]; we were doing practically as we liked. We soon left the village some distance behind us, and it was now pitch dark and very cold, altho' it was very hot by day, so some of the lads got fed up and decided to halt on their own. Well they did so, and I expect that's how some of them found themselves prisoners of war. Nearly half of our little lot went and sat at the roadside, and about 15 or 20 of us decided to stick it till we came across some of our own troops or someone who could sort us out, as mind you reader, we were in a strange country, and were practically strangers to each other as we had come off the Reserve only a few days before, and for all we knew Fritz might be waiting for us at any bend or corner of that country road. So what would you have done? The same as us I expect, which was the same as Felix did. We eventually arrived at a big chateau, which to us seemed like a castle in the dark, and we could hear the rattle of horses' bits, and the stamping of horses' feet in the yard surrounded by some outbuildings. We could see a big gate under an archway, and could also see the flash of somebody's big guns away to our right. One of my mates banged on the gate with his rifle, and a voice inside yelled "Hullo, who the hells that?" and we knew we found British troops. It turned out to be the same cavalry patrol that had warned us back in the village. They had a young officer with them and about a dozen horses, but only about six or eight men, so we knew they had had a skirmish with Fritz somewhere and had come away with a few empty saddles. They had a fire going and a bucket of some sort was filled up with all sorts of a mixture, fowls, rabbits, etc, as I remember saying to one of them that that was jut the sort of stew up we had had at the place where they warned us overnight. The French civvies were still living in this chateau place, and as they knew that Fritz would probably be there the next day, they had given this cavalry patrol a free hand. I can still see some tea being made in a rusty bucket. Any old how, we were invited to "muck in "and we soon got some of that stew, as the motto over there was, at the start of the war, to eat all you possibly could while you were able, as you never knew when you would get the next meal, or if you would ever get another one. So after another "blow out" [and as we had some French "tabac" given by the people in the house to make fags with], we had a smoke and got down to finish our sleep some miles away from the place where we started it.

It seemed as tho' we had only been asleep five minutes [but we really had no idea of time by then], when we were roused by the cavalry patrol once more. They had already fed and watered their horses, and were ready to move off. The officer gave one of us some instructions as to the route to take as far as he knew would be safe, and away they went on their "hosses". We were on our own once more. As there did not seem to be any war on just in our locality, somebody suggested "drumming up", [making some tea] before we pushed off. So as we were all agreeable we "drummed up". We "busted open" our iron rations of tea and sugar, and put them all together in the bucket. Then we "scrounged" some bread and butter from the civvies living in the chateau, and that with some "bully beef" made our breakfast to start off another day of what was going to be a four year's struggle. It's a lucky job for us that the civvies were still in the house, I think, as we may not have had that breakfast.

After we finished the meal we got away on the route given to us by the officer of the cavalry patrol, and taking into consideration that all the blinking Fritz army was somewhere about, to say nothing of the French and British, it was surprising us that we met no troops of any sort for a couple of hours. It was not long after dawn, remember, when we were out of it. For all we knew we might have been behind the German lines, and one or two little incidents that occurred made me think more than once that we were. Sometimes we heard firing straight in front of us, and then again, we saw shells bursting away on our left front whereas the German army was supposed to be on our right rear as far as we knew. I tell you we were in a fix, and the only thing we could do was keep walking to prevent getting captured. As I say, after about a couple of hours marching we sighted some cavalry away on a slope that was right in front, and we thought "now we're getting somewhere". Just near us was a bit of a cutting in the road and as we marched along into it, these cavalry came hell for leather towards us yelling and waving swords. Up to that time we had never seen any French cavalry so of course when we saw this crowd of about 30 charging towards us we naturally thought it was German cavalry. We jumped to the side of the road facing them, loaded our rifles, and lay on the bank determined to let them have it hot when they got near enough. They had helmets on like fireman wear in England and black plumes of hair flying out behind them as they tore across the fields at us. I don't know why to this day we did not shoot, but somehow we didn't, and when they got within about 100 yards of us one of them flung his arm in the air with his sword gripped tight and they pulled up just on the bank over us. It was explained to us that seeing us coming along that road and then disappearing into that bit of a cutting they thought we were Fritz's troops going to open fire at them. The one who had stopped the charge had been in England quite a lot he told us, and as they galloped towards us he recognised our khaki. He could speak English well, and so we had a talk with him as to where to go for our best route. He admitted that they were charging us with intention of making mincemeat of us, thinking we were Fritzs in the distance, and we retaliated by politely telling him that if we had opened fire on them they would have stood no earthly chance of getting near us. So we all had a laugh and a few jokes together, after he had interpreted to his pals what we had said. I have found out since that they were "Chasseurs". Well he put us wise to the fact that if we kept going in the same direction as we were going we would soon have some Uhlans [German cavalry] after us, as they had just finished a scrap with some Uhlans over there when they spotted us, and thought they would get their own back. He advised us to leave the road and strike across country to our left, and sooner or later we should, with some luck, come to Le "something" [I suppose now he meant Le Cateau[10], but I didn't know then]. So after a few more jokes and much polite chaff at the funny dress of them, we pushed across country and the "Entente Cordiale" was made a bit stronger; but if we fired the old "15 rounds a minute rapid", like we did at Fritz the day before, France would have lost some of her Chasseurs. So that was another little episode of the Great War ended. [I wouldn't mind if they all ended up like that.]

We were on our own once again and we began to worry if all the British Army except ourselves were dead or gone home, and what the time was, and how far this "Le" or "St" something was away, and how far Fritz was away, or where he was, and a host of other things, as we struggled along across country. It's a good job there were no hedges to climb over, like there are in England, as we might have given it up. After about an hours tracking we came across a battery of our 18 pounders with their muzzles facing into our direction waiting for a bang at Fritz, so we were evidently on the right path at last, although I believe now if it had not been for those "Chasers" we should have finished up in Berlin, as our 18 pounders opened fire at some Fritz as we walked towards them. We asked if any of our troops were about, and were told that an officer of our lot and a party of men passed the battery about half an hour previous, and that they better beat it quick as they were firing at some Uhlans then.

We eventually overtook our old Major Prowse and a sergeant and about 40 men halted in a wood. After a rest, and much relating of experiences, and munching of biscuits [army pattern] we all fell in together and marched off under our old Major once more. Quids in! In due course we

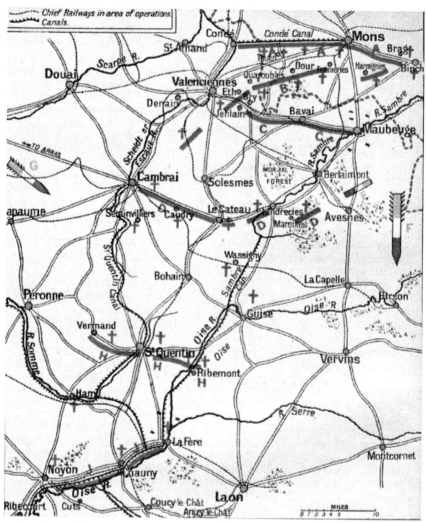

1st phase of Retreat from Mons. British positions 23rd–28th August 1914

arrived at St Quentin[11] the place that the French cavalry patrol had spoken off, and there met a lot of troops of our Brigade and other Brigades who had concentrated there. A lot of sorting out had to be done very quickly, and some grub was served out from the transport there and we were off again towards Paris. I just can't remember where we met the remains of our regiment or what was left of them, as different little parties of stragglers came joining up from different parts most every day on that long trek to

"Paree", and we were beginning to get quite a respectable "gang" together again. I say "gang" because this was all we had been for a couple of days. Well now we had lost count of days and hours, as we had never had any regular times for meals or sleep or any other old thing during the retreat from Mons. Day was turned into night, night into day, Sunday the same as any other day if there was a "scrap" to be had. Sleep when we could, which was very seldom, and the same with feeding. Very hot by day, and cold at night, day after day, night after night, the same old thing, left, right, left. By crumbs!

First German attempts at trench and bunker building in the early part of the War.
Note that the German soldiers are still wearing Pickelhauben..
[The Prussian spiked helmet was worn by troops from the 19th century onwards.
The word derives from Pickel [point] and Haube [bonnet]. Although worn at the start
of the Great War, it was soon discovered that it was not suitable for trench warfare,
offering very little protection from shrapnel. From the beginning of 1916 it was slowly
replaced by a steel helmet [Stahlheim]. The spiked helmet remained the mental
image of the German soldier in allied eyes.

CHAPTER 5

The Retreat Towards Paris: The Forest of Compiègne

One day we arrived at a big forest, which I learnt was the "Forest of Compiègne". It had long straight roads running through, as straight as arrows, where we met heaps of British troops. Generals, Colonels, Brigade Majors, Staff Captains, and all sorts of different "nobs", Artillery, Cavalry, Infantry and Staff motor cars and lorries of "grub" were all bivouacked in the forest. We had a really long halt there and were able to strip and hang out shirts on branches to air a bit [they needed airing too], as we only had what we stood up in which was the same shirt as we put on about a week before we left England. As we had done some fighting and rushing about in the heat, and long marches since we started mind you, of course our poor old feet were beginning to ask for a chance, as our boots had not been off since we left the camp in Havre on the Sunday. So shirts were peeled off, likewise putties and socks in the glorious shade of the forest, and if Fritz's Uhlans had made a swoop they would have captured a few dozen naked troops. Our feet were raw and in some cases the skin of the lad's feet had peeled off with their socks and were bleeding. Blisters were common everywhere. What a relief to get our boots off even if only for a couple of hours, relief yes! But, by crumbs, what a stink too. Sweaty shirts and socks, sweaty bodies and feet. No wonder someone said, "put them all on again, or we shall kill all the trees, and then Fritz will see us". Well later we did have to "put 'em on" again, and oh what a struggle. Our feet had swollen during that couple of hours halt so that it was murder to drive them back into our boots again, and when we got on the move again the first few miles were simply agony till our "poor old feet" got climatised again.

Well now I said were sorted out a bit at a time and had the Colonel back again, Col. Swayne. I believe, though I can't be certain, that Capt Sutton,

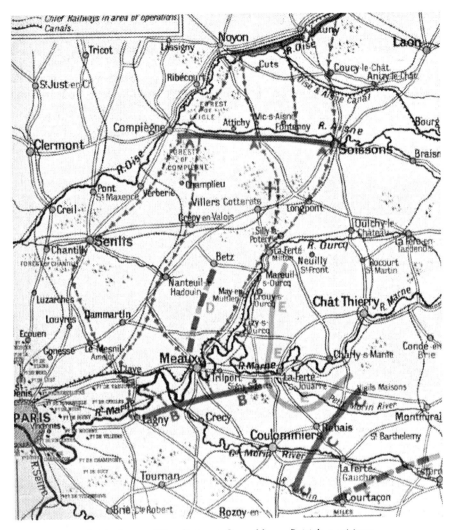

2nd phase of the Retreat from Mons. British positions
28th August 1914–6th September 1914

the Adjutant, was also there. I know Brigadier-General Hunter-Watson was in charge of the remnants of our Brigade, as we were getting quite ship-shape now and swinging along through the forest for miles. Really it's some forest, and we came to the end of it near a little village called St Sauveur. We halted in the village for, as we thought, the usual "ten minutes" halt, fell out on the left of the road, but as the time went by, and no signs of "fall in" appeared rumours started flying about, such rumours as

"We've come the wrong way", or "The war's over", and again "We are surrounded by the Germans". All helped to make it more exciting. The last rumour was nearest; as General Hunter-Watson came riding up through the village, and as he got opposite to where I was sprawled on my back in the ditch, he said these words, which I shall forever remember. He said "There is a chance to get a bit of your own back boys, as there are a few German cavalry up in front cut off from their main body". Of course we had been issued out afresh with plenty of ammunition during our stay in the forest, and we had also had a rest and a couple of feeds, so we were ready for a cut at Fritz any old time.

We fell in on the village road and moved ahead to some high ground overlooking the village and forest we had just left, and lined the edge of a gully. About 300 or 400 yards across the village from our direction came sounds of shouting and yelling and sniping, with an occasional rattle of a machine gun. Now we did not mind so much now we knew where to look for trouble, but the worst part of a job of that sort was looking for the enemy without knowing where he was, and not knowing whether you were going to get it in the back. We lay along the edge of this gully loaded up, and watching for any signs of Fritz's cavalrymen. One of my pals had looted a pair of field glasses from somewhere during the retreat, and I asked for a "squint" through them [by the way those glasses were the means of saving a Fritz's life, as I'll show you later on]. On taking the glasses and hearing some sniping from the direction of the wood, I looked in that direction, and low down on the ground at the edge of the wood I could see flashes of their rifles. I told the Sergeant, who also had a pair, of what I could see, and after he had made sure through his own glasses, he gave us the range and orders thus "500 yards, and fire 5 rounds at the edge of the wood". We opened fire and then using the glasses again we could see them dashing through the trees towards their horses. They were all big hefty chaps and as they hurried back up the wooded slopes so well did their uniform of grey-green blend with the surroundings, that it was impossible to see them without glasses when they were still. There I saw my first Uhlans.

The Sergeant told us to let them have a few more rounds before they went, so we all fired again, and just afterwards we saw about a dozen riderless horses gallop madly from the wood so we knew we had not wasted "ammo". Then we saw a little party of our own troops running from the direction of the wood, and as some of them were limping we guessed that

that was what the Uhlans had been firing at, so we gave them a few more "parting shots" and then had orders to "cease fire" and be quiet. While we lay there waiting for further orders, four shells screamed over our heads and "plonked" in the ground about 200 yards behind us . [I did not know Uhlans carried field guns about with them on their saddles!.]Later on in the war that particular kind of shell got the nickname of the "whiz-bang". Things quietened down again, and we had orders to form up near a farm about half a mile away, and it was there that we learnt that instead of a "Few Uhlans cut off from their main body", as the "Gen" had told us, it was a good try on Fritz's part to cut us off from our main body and plenty of light field guns were sighted by our cavalry scouts. Still we had all sorts of yarns told in those days, to keep our "peckers up" I guess.

I well recollect now one yarn in particular that was being continually rammed down our gills. It was to the effect that as we had done so well at Mons and since then, we were going to have a long rest when we reached the forts that encircled Paris, which we should do in a few days [with luck]. Of course stuff like that is good medicine to keep troops on the go. Anyway after putting paid to Fritz in that little skirmish, we dropped back into the old routine left, right, left along these dreary, dusty country roads, or cutting across country sometimes, till we eventually crossed the river Aisne and still kept on "Felixing". It was a case of the old song "We don't know where we're going but when we get there we'll be glad". All day long and into the night with only occasional halts. Any little check up front used to make us coming up behind halt, and the troops used to flop down like "dead mutton" just where they stood, and were sound asleep before they hit the ground. I well remember once dropping on the cobble stones during a hold up and was woken up by someone banging me on the dial with his flat hand and yelling "Wake up, Wake up, the Germans are on us". A bit more bunk to get us on the move! One good thing about it now was that Fritz was not warning us quite so much since that smack in the eye at St Sauvier, but I believe if he had come on he would have made some captives, as we were almost too whacked to stand let alone shoot. Then again I expect if we had been overtaken by him, we should have pulled that little bit extra which is in everyone when they are "up against it", and have given Fritz another taste of our shooting. Naturally there was plenty of "cussing and grousing" as that is the only privilege a Tommy has, also, many a time the remarks was passed when Fritz was supposed to be on us, "Oh let them come, we shall get a damned sleep if we are captured".

CHAPTER **6**

The Marne and the Aisne

We hadn't had a square meal now for sometime, years it seemed, and one day we came to the river Marne and crossed it, and still kept on going ahead, snatching a nap or some sorts of grub, just when and how we could. I really cannot tell the date of when we crossed the Marne or the River Aisne, but I know we arrived at a place called Lagny inside the ring of forts, which we had heard so much about, on September 5th. So, from the 22nd August till that day we had been marching and fighting, hot, cold, hungry, thirsty, tired, footsore and weary, but still game.

Thirteen days before we had left the rain at Le Cateau, and now we were at the gates of Paris.

We thought we were really right for a long rest after all. The optimists said, "There, what did we tell you," but the pessimists said, "Garn, we shall shove on again as soon as we've had some grub". We were put in the grounds of a big Chateau, with orders not to touch the fruit and vegetables. I ask you. Tomatoes were growing in abundance, so as I'm very partial to tomatoes, my mouth watered, but not for long [they tasted lovely too]. The transport arrived, and a huge fire was soon made in the grounds. Dixies of water were soon turned into tea. Bread and Butter [all capital letters please], Tea with Milk and Sugar, and then a Stew was made after that with real Meat and Spuds, Carrots, and [local grown] Tomatoes. Oh it was grand, lovely, glorious, I could have ate for a year. Then some fags were served out. "Fags" what you smoke mind, a packet each, and wasn't it grand to feel the smoke going into your mouth after that feed and as we hadn't had a smoke for days, I can taste them now. Well after a good old honest to goodness "blow out" we were told we should sleep in some stables, there among the straw, but no blankets, of course, and get after

Fritz in the morning, as you will remember that which is now history, of how Fritz was turned back at the very gates of Paris, and so we had to see that he kept going.

The long rest, which we had been promised, had to be postponed. So we had the one night's sleep in the straw with boots off and were told we should parade in a little wood, which ran around the chateau grounds, sometime next day for "kit inspection" by the Colonel as he did not want to see any "loot". Ye Gods, a kit inspection, mind you! Why we hadn't any kit barring a rifle, bayonet, equipment, razor and towel and some ammunition. How we laughed at the thought of it. Anyhow we paraded next day some time in the wood in our different companies with what we had laid out on the moss and dead leaves. I can see that kit now. Some had a haversack filled with tomatoes or apples, some with bully and biscuits, others with nothing but their rifle, equipment and "ammo". The "loot" part of the inspection was soon overcome as those who had "won" anything simply buried it under the leaves where they stood. However the "kit inspection" yarn was simply a ruse to get us there, as British troops are noted for discipline [as I'll show you in a minute], and of course, giving orders for a "kit inspection" sounded more regimental than merely saying the Colonel wanted to talk to us. He did not inspect kit, but he did talk to us, and if he had heard what was said about him when he had finished "spouting", and what some of the lads would like you do to him, he would have gone back to England by the next boat. However in less than a week he had left us for England with "shattered nerves", so maybe someone told him a few of the remarks after all, and that may have "shattered" them for him; but I certainly do not think they were "shattered" when he was "talking" to us. I remember thinking to myself that he had a blinking hard nerve talking as he did. Anyway let me tell you as near as possible what he said. He led off by saying what great deeds we had performed "in action", and how we had given the Germans a taste of our fighting abilities which had been the cause of them thinking twice before they attacked British troops in a hurry, "ahem", and how proud the "brass hats" were of us and all that, and that it would go down in the pages of history etc. etc. three bags full. [I remember thinking at the time of those words of the Duke of Wellington or Charlie Chaplin, I forget which, but I know it was some retired admiral words to this effect, "What will they say of this in England?"] Well now after rubbing us all up the right way with those pretty little words, the silly old man turned right round and went off the deep end. He said, "Remember discipline and discipline alone has brought you here, and without discipline you would have become a rabble. Look at you, there is hardly a cap badge or a shoulder ornament among you etc. etc. Now reader I ask you to take into consideration the fact that the French lassies in that camp at Havre on that Sunday in August had loaded us with fruit and sweets and wine ect etc. Wasn't it only natural that they should effect some souvenir in return, also were we not amongst the first divisions to go to France and of course the French people were pleased to see us, and made a fuss of us? Well that's where the cap badges etc went. Also taking into consideration that we had had at the very start two or three days hard fighting, marched for days and nights on end and had a few more skirmishes with Fritz, stood there in the same clothes and shirt as we left England in, hadn't had a real good wash for several days, had been hungry, thirsty, hot, cold, tired, footsore and weary for many a day, would any man, unless his nerves were shattered, expect troops to be of the same smartness as they would be, say, on a Church parade? We had done all that we had been asked to do, viz fight and kill Germans. We killed them in hundreds, and now here was the old man "rearing up" because we had got ourselves dirty and untidy doing it. Of course we understood what the "old cock" was getting at us, us having the usual share of Tommie's intellect, but at the same time, much as I admired the way this "Mr Discipline" had brought us all the way from Mons to the outskirts of Paris, I really could not help thinking that my poor old feet had a good share in my getting there. Still, as I am always ready to thank anyone what does me a good turn, after the "talking to and at" had finished, I hunted round for this Mr Discipline to say "thank you very much, shut the gate as you go out", and as I could not find him I came to the conclusion that he must have died of heart failure, after lugging us all that distance; so I gave it up. However we were told to dismiss, then our old Major [Major Prowse] had a little chat with us on his own.

What a contrast in the two men's speeches. The poor old Major guessed that such a "lecture" as the Colonel had given us was sticking in our gills, and it was, believe me reader, so he spoke to us like a father. He said something similar to the Colonel as regards our fighting abilities and general good work "in action", our steadfastness under fire etc. etc. Thank you very much and he said that General French was going to pat our backs when he met us, yes please. Then he went on to say that the French army

The much loved Major Prowse, later
Brigadier-General

had succeeded in turning the Germans back from Paris, and had them "on the run", and that our jobs now were to get 'em and keep them on the run till they got back to Germany. He also said that if any man had done something great and it was brought to his notice, he would write to that man's village and tell them all about it, but also if any man showed the "white feather" he would also write to that man's village and let them know all about it too.

So we had two choices in the fighting that was to come. But the Major's little talk to us [not at us], put us in a better humour than the Colnel's miserable words did, and it goes to show the different types of officer of the "Old Contemptible Army".

Bridge on the Marne

Well that same day we had to start tracking again, this time away from Paris and after Fritz. [The date now is September 6th, and it's about the first chance I've had to get a correct date since we started on the railway train at Le Cateau on August 22nd.] We marched away towards the River Marne from the Paris direction and my second view of the Marne was at a place called La Ferte, where we found that the Fritz's had blown up the bridge to prevent us crossing, and the Field Company, Royal Engineers had lost a lot of men putting a pontoon bridge across under fire. We were posted about in the woods overlooking the fort and our orders were to pick off Fritzs we could see in the valley. We did not see many about and only had to fire a few rounds once at a little bunch running along the railway bank. We saw two drop and their pals pulled one away and left one. I suppose he was dead. We hung about in the woods till nearly dark, waiting for orders. It was fairly quiet, only an occasional rattle of machine guns somewhere and a bit of sniping going on in our locality, but there was a certain machine gun posted somewhere on the hill across the river that was a damned nuisance. He could not see us in the woods, and we took it for granted that it was a Fritz machine gun party that had been left behind with orders to hold on as long as possible. He must have been well blessed with "ammo" and wanted to get rid of it, as every few minutes he would fire off a drum, and swing his gun as he was firing it. Of course the darned bullets would be sprayed all over the place, so we had to keep pretty low while he was "acting the fool" with his gun. I know many of us there said "I'd like to be behind that square headed —— while he's firing that gun!"

When it was almost dark, the Sergeant of my platoon, Sgt Todd, was told to take his platoon down to the pontoon bridge over the river and report to the officer of Field Coy RE's. He formed us up and away we went through the wooded slopes of the Marne Valley till we arrived at the bridge. He found the officer in charge and had orders from him to do outpost duty on the pontoon bridge for the night [we had a snip]. There wasn't anything really to do but hang about, just in case Fritz or any of the French civvies tried to pinch the bridge. We waited around till all the rest of the column had crossed the river and, by the way, our pals who had to go on and keep marching didn't forget to call us a few names. [Lucky — and so forth!]. Sgt Todd told us off in reliefs for "sentry go", and those not actually on sentry, myself included, started on the scrounge. There were about eight or ten of us, and I think as near as I remember it was about the second or third day since we left the chateau near Paris. By the time we had found a camping space at the end of the bridge on the far side of the river, and after we had got some timber and water and a fire going, it was dark, and, having bagged a "dixie" [camp kettle] from the transport column as they passed over, and some rations, we soon made ourselves as comfortable as we could for the night seated round the old camp fire of England; home and reality. [Perhaps.] Well, after getting "down to it" till my turn came to go on sentry sometime during the night, which was two hours of walking backwards and forwards across the bridge from one bank to another, we were suddenly roused soon after day break from our slumbers round the fire by a big fat Frenchman rushing into our little camp yelling something. Now it was rather a mad thing to do, only he did not know it, but to wake a bunch of British Tommies up when they are nice and comfortable is not the "correct thing" if you want them to be polite and pleasant. So I think he was greeted with something like "What the H—l is the matter with thee; go away you big Frog-scoffing, etc.etc." But he would not go away. He stood there shouting and semaphoring with his arms and pointed up the road saying something that sounded like "Bosh". So, of course someone had to say "I know it's Bosh so why doesn't he shut up?" But Sgt Todd said we had better go and see what's up. He sent three of us, including myself along with the old Froggie, and put me in charge, as he used to say I was the best "scrounger" he had ever met and this might be a chance to bring back some poultry or something for breakfast. So off I set with my two trusty pals. Wait a minute though. We were starting off without rifles or anything else. But Froggie pointed to our guns and jabbered some more about the "Bosh" stuff, [I learned later that "Boche", which of course sounded like "Bosh" to our ears was French for German, etc.], so I said "Let's take our guns and "ammo" and we picked our guns. Poor old Froggie looked ever so relieved and pleased so we guessed there was going to be some dirty work at the crossroads [as us three brave souls started off to stop the invasion of France]. Ahem! We didn't know what the devil we were in for and if old Von Kluck and all his army were waiting at the corner for us, as there were only three of us, and about half dozen more back at the bridge, to fall back on. [Such is the stuff heroes are made of.] However we went back up the road towards the town of La Ferte with a bodyguard, which consisted of the big fat Frenchie and a load of women and kiddies who had run down to meet my army and me. We met some more Frenchies on the way up and, of course, everyone was trying to tell us three all about it in French, and as they did not learn me to talk French at school I would answer "Oh I see", "Alright" and such like. I began to feel like somebody of some importance I tell you. Was I not in charge of the British army of two? Did not the honour of the whole of the Allies rest upon my field service cap, part worn size 6 7/8th, but felt much larger. Not 'alf. Anyway our big fat guide led us to a monastery where we saw some nuns who spoke English. They handed over to me four of the prettiest little Fritzs you could wish for, and informed us that there was some more wounded ones inside. Having gone over the building and searched it thoroughly to make sure there were no more spare parts of Fritz's army knocking around, I came back to the nun, or nurse, whoever she was, and she told us that the Fritzs had bolted in there the day before during the fighting around the town, and when they had thought all the

British troops had gone after them, they showed themselves early that morning [little did they know that me and my army of two was knocking around]. We decided that, as we could not put the 8 or 9 wounded in our haversacks, we would take all the rifles and bayonets and ammunition away from them, and get back with the four alive and kicking ones. They also had a spare box of ammunition, so we made those four carry that and loaded them up with the rifles and bayonets etc., and started off back to our little camp at the bridgehead, to the accompaniment of "hisses and boos" which were, of course, meant for Fritz. We arrived and reported to the Sgt and had orders to smash up the rifles and dump them with the ammunition in the river, which we did. So. If you want a souvenir "de la guerre" just go out to La Ferte on the Marne, and on the side further from Paris you might fish out some rusty rifles and bayonets.

Having received no orders about moving off we were at liberty to roam around a bit, so telling Sgt Todd I was going out to have a scrounge for anything that was going, a pal and I set out. We purposely took the same direction as we had previously been to fetch the Fritzs as we got near to the houses. I was recognised as the "bloke" who had called for the rent [beg pardon I mean the prisoners], and I was made very welcome thank you, by the civvies of La Ferte. I had, I think, about five spare packets of tobacco given me, good stuff for making fags, some fag papers, bread, I think two loaves long ones shaped like submarines, some champion butter and some eggs, besides sitting down in some posh lady's house and having a feed of egg and chips, coffee and milk, followed by some wine and grapes. We were in clover as you see those people were overjoyed to think that our troops had driven Fritz through the town without having the chance to do much damage to property and human beings. They would have given us anything. The house we were entertained in was a picture in itself. The carpets we walked on in our dirty, dusty boots must have cost enough to furnish an ordinary working man's home, and when we had sat down on the chairs we nearly sank down a mile before we stopped. After blowing ourselves out, we gathered all the spares of bread, eggs, butter etc, and bidding the lady good morning in plain English, we set out back to let the other lads have a feed. A couple more had been out in another direction so they had arrived with more grub and we had enough to have a meal at dinner. We spent another night there, and next morning we received orders to go on the move again. The Sergeant was given instructions as to the route, etc., as we had been at the bridge two nights and a day, and the main body must be well away by then. So after being put wise we set out with our four prisoners for the River Aisne.

The Aisne

It was somewhere between the River Marne and the Aisne that I saw the old Colonel in a Red Brass wagon en route for England with his "shattered nerves". We had lost count of days and dates again and had no mail from England up to that time, and I know I was surprised when we did finally reach the Aisne to find out it was the 14th of September. So you see, it took us 8 days to get from just outside Paris to the hills of the Aisne Valley. The river had been crossed under heavy fire and the bridge where we arrived was only partially blown up so some 18 pounder guns were being manhandled across when we came up. I must mention here our little band took no part in the actual fighting at the river itself, as the main body had crossed a couple of days before, but we were on the hills, just across the valley of the river, and the bridge was actually being shelled by Fritz guns when we came up. The valley was rather wide, and Fritz as you know now had dug himself in on the heights on the far side and as it turned out was settled there for two or three years. We had handed over our prisoners somewhere en route, and were now drawing near to our own main body. When we arrived at our own broken bridge, we had orders from the officer on duty there to dash across in twos and threes between the salvoes of Fritz shells, and scatter for cover as soon as we reached the far side. [I'm glad it was not a very long bridge.]

There were several dead artillery pals lying around under groundsheets awaiting burial, so signs that like that always gave us the tip whether a place was healthy or otherwise. We obeyed orders and dashed across the bridge just as Fritz burst four very big shells overhead, and scrambled to earth like foxes on the far side to wait for the others. We had the luck to all get over without anyone "stopping a lump of shell", and I well remember crouching low over there as we had to wait for the darkness before crossing about a mile of very flat and absolutely open country to where our troops were entrenched on the hillside near the village of Bucy-le-Long[12], not far from Soissons. So we crouched about a quarter of a mile from the bridge and watched Fritz shelling it with "Jack Johnsons"[13] and

"Shrapnel". When they considered it was dark enough we got on the move across the Aisne valley, and up into the hills till we were challenged by a sentry saying, "Halt! Who goes there?" Seeing who we were, we were directed up through a fir tree wood, and eventually found the regiment's headquarters in some caves up there in the hills. A big fire was going in the mouth of one of the caves and it looked quite homely. My old Major [Major Prowse] who had taken on the colonel's job was talking to Sgt Major Paul [afterwards promoted to Captain, but who was killed in September 1918]. We had some stew served out to us there and then were told to join our company somewhere in some holes, somewhere over there in the wood; some instructions eh! Well anyhow, we found 'em and were then told by Company Sergeant Major Gauge [I think that's how it's spelt], to dig some holes for ourselves "in that bank at the edge of the wood". What a splendid reception for us who had captured half the German Army [4 men], and we had come all the way from Paris to pay him a visit. I think we decided among ourselves that the Company Sgt-Major's holes could go to that warm place which we have all heard of, and so we just flopped down as we were and waited for tomorrow.

We had no trouble with our bedclothes, as our great coats were all the bedclothes we possessed in those days. We sat huddled up together for warmth talking and dozing till dawn broke, and incidentally with the dawn came a salvo of Fritz's shrapnel just over us into the wood, which nearly ended the war for some of us, but not quite. The lads who had arrived before us told us that was the usual morning salute from Fritz, and soon after a battery of our guns in the valley behind us returned the compliment. Now I am able to give a few dates once more, as we appear to have been brought to a standstill owing to the fact that while a large army of Fritz's troops had gone on to get to Paris, another of his spare armies had dug themselves in at some quarries[14] near the River Aisne and was easily able to hold our depleted forces. That's how we were informed at the time anyhow. Well we arrived here yesterday as it were, and today is the 15th September 1914. We were told that we should likely remain here for a while so to prepare some shelter for ourselves from shellfire and winter weather. That sounded hopeful any old how. We all had our special pals by now, so I had a pal named Cook, off the reserve, and him and I got our entrenching tools busy and dug our way into the earth at the foot of a good sized tree. On down under the roots we went hard at it and by a day's hard work we had a good-sized hole down in the chalk. After about a day there the majority of us were fairly safe from shellfire unless we had a direct hit on the bank with a big'un, and then we should have "resided permanently in France, no flowers by request" RIP.

From the 15th September till the 6th October things were more or less the same each day and night, and ran on these lines. Dawn would break and with the dawn would come Fritz's morning salute, a salvo of shrapnel, and after a suitable pause our guns would reply. Then we would get some "breakfast" somehow, and crawl back into our "rabbit holes" to eat it and wait for anything that might turn up in the shape of mail from England, or rations of fags or anything to relieve the monotony. For the first couple of days we were not very well fed, but as the transport facilities were improved so did our diet, and one day a big chunk of beef was found to have "worked it's passage" from HQs and was lying on a sack near our hole. We set about that like vultures round a dead "hoss" in the desert, and our jack knives and bayonets soon hacked it to death. We used to go scrounging down to the gardens of the houses in the village of Bucy and loot spuds and artichokes etc, and when this chunk of dead hoss arrived we had a steak and chips for dinner, steak like leather, and chips burnt to a cinder, still what wasn't fattening was filling, and by the time we moved from the wood I had actually put on weight.

One day while there, with for nothing else better to do, I wandered off down to the gardens of the village to get some of these artichokes, which they were all "winning" [and someone was losing]. Now I was not found under a gooseberry bush when I was a babe, consequently I had not learnt much about greengrocery, and when I arrived at the gardens I saw a chap pulling carrots. As I had already searched around for these "darned chokes" and couldn't find any, I said to the "carrot puller", "Hi kid where's these blinking "aunty-chokes" everybody's eating up on the hill"? At the time I was standing close to some very tall stems like sunflower stems. So he answered "If they stalks give way what thee bist leaning against, thee bist going to fall down on 'em". How was I to know they had "gert long stalks" like that, me not having been born under a "goosy bush". Besides I thought that "uncle-chokes" were things one bought in greengrocers shops. I didn't know they grew [liar].

Another day a Fritz plane came over and flew rather leisurely up and down our lines. Our anti-aircraft guns at that time were nothing to write home about. We had a pom-pom there which I think must have been used to fire at aircraft in the Crimean War [if they had any then], and it certainly put up a goodish show at making pretty little clouds of smoke in the air with it's shells, but the shells always burst where Fritz wasn't [still, well done the gunners]. The plane came over and then flew back to its own lines. Soon after he had gone back, Fritz sent over a few heavy shells down in the valley somewhere, and then the plane came over again to "spot" for his gunners. Well to make a long story short. Old Fritz's guns made a proper mess of a battery of our guns down in the valley on that September morn, and we did not have any reply to Fritz's good morning salvo the next day. Some of our chaps got a bit pessimistic and said such things as "We shall lose the war", and "Now Fritz will come over and drive us right back t'other side of Paris", etc. etc. [but we didn't and he didn't]; although I sometimes wonder whether we gained any advantage in winning the war. Another day two French 75s [guns] were brought up and put in position just in front of the wood where we had dug our rabbit holes. They fired about a 100 rounds and then limbered up and galloped away. We thought perhaps they had put that battery out which had knocked our battery about and was congratulating ourselves on being more secure when all of a sudden Fritz "let go" right into us all along the edge of the wood. My word readers it was Hell with the lid off for about half an hour. Big shells and shrapnel all crashing among the trees and shaking up the earth like an earthquake. I suppose old Fritz must have thought our guns were just inside the woods under cover after firing but they had gone. We had to stand the brunt of Fritz's temper. The result was for us, I heard, Lt's Newton and Read and several men were killed and wounded. Didn't we cuss those French guns. The very next day the same two guns were brought up again to repeat the dose, and Fritz was waiting for them, and while they were actually firing Fritz fired bang into them killing several gunners and wounding some and killing two or three horses in the wood which we had to bury when they began to "buzz" a bit.

On the 17th September I had a parcel from home. Included in it were some apples; apples, mind you, and we had practically eaten our way from Mons to Paris on apples and pears etc. Still they didn't know that, poor people. On the 26th September I had another parcel and made a grand tea for my pals that day; cake and jam and fried spuds. I had just finished boiling a canteen of water when four shells came over for extras. Several had the hard lines of getting hit. The shell cases that the French gunners left behind made lovely fire grates for our canteens, by driving them into the earth and lodging our canteens across them. That's about all we had to thank those guns for, as I always think they were the means of us getting shelled regularly every day after that.

One day we received orders that we were going out at night to dig a trench across our front, as the ground out in front gradually sloped upwards so that we could not see more than 500 or 600 yards to our front. So the "Brass Hats" decided on a lot of night trench digging to keep us warm. Every thing in the garden was lovely for the first night, but when daylight came and Fritz saw this brand new trench right under their noses, as it were, he knew what we had been up to during the night. He did not shell it though as he naturally thought it was unoccupied, but he knew we should be where he wanted us when it got dark again at night. So he saved his shells for us. As I say, he knew what we had been up to, and we knew what he would be up to later, but Fritz was just too late for once. Just as I thought, so it panned out, only we did not parade for digging just when Fritz thought we might. We moved out from the wood and were just a few yards from the trench when he sent about a dozen shells screaming over our heads. Had he been about three minutes earlier he would have caught us lovely between the wood and trench without a blade of grass for cover. We dug some more that night and again the next, till we were getting quite a respectable trench, but I suppose the old saying "familiarity breeds contempt" could very well be inserted here. As Fritz seemed to be ignoring our presence, the "Heads" decided to alter the digging time to allow the officer in charge [Captain Bradshaw killed in action December 1914], to report what the trench looked like in daylight, or at dawn anyway. So we paraded about midnight to go out and dig till about 4am and then all to get in the trench under cover and keep down while the officer walked around to inspect the work done. That was the orders as we had them. All went according to plan. 4am came; we stopped digging and got in the trench, and away went Capt Bradshaw. But either the job took longer than the "Heads" thought it would, or else he might have met some of his pals somewhere up the trench, as it was broad daylight before he joined us. He looked out over the trench just near to where I was sitting to look around, and he spotted some bundles of clover lying out there in front about 100 yards away, which I suppose the farmer had cut ready for loading when he had to flee away from the Hun. He turned to me and said "You" and "You", pointing to another chap, jump out there and get a couple of bundles of that stuff and scatter it over some of the chalk here to cover it up a bit. Orders being orders we had a push up the trench side and dashed across to these bundles of clover. We got the bundles alright one under each arm and were coming back with them as fast as we were able, but seeing as it was broad daylight by now, and Fritz could see us, he must have thought we had a hard neck pinching the farmer's clover; so he let us know what he thought of us with a burst of machine gun fire. I did not stop to argue with him, nor did the other bloke, but we dropped the bundles about 30 yards from the trench and dropped into it with these darned bullets tearing up the ground around; no rabbits have ever shot into their holes quicker than my mate and I dived into that trench. After we had cooled down it was a laugh all round, and no one knew if we were hit or not for a minute or so, but it was no laughing matter to be sprinting with bundles of clover and Fritz urging you on with these machine guns. I reckon it was the nearest squeak I had had for a while, and I may say that the chalk itself did not get covered up that morning. As I said before it was daylight now, and there we were, about 40 or 50 of us stuck in a trench out in the middle of a field in full view of Fritz as soon as we stuck our noses above the parapet. Put yourselves in our place and think what to do. We couldn't stay there all day till it was dark again as Fritz had only to turn up his big guns on us to wipe us off the map, as we were only down about 5 feet, just an ordinary trench cut straight across a field and about 500 or 600 yards away from our holes in the woods. We expected Fritz to "let rip" any minute now he knew the trench was occupied.

Well this is how we got away. Capt Bradshaw gave orders for us to get out of the trench in twos and threes and sprint like hell for the woods. Two men had had to get out at one end of the trench, and two or three at the other end, then a couple in the centre and so on. Mind you each man had the rifle and straps and either a pick or a shovel to carry. The first two or three pals got away all right but when Fritz tumbled to the game he soon let us know he was fully awake with his machine gun. So those of us who were still waiting our turn knew we were for it when our turn came to dash. As each pair or three dashed away the others would peep over the parapet to see how they got on; one went down smack during the rush and we said "that's one", but he was up and gone like a gazelle; he found later that a bullet had gone clean through his haversack strapped to his back. He said he felt at the time as though someone had punched him in the kidneys, so he let himself fall. Well I knew as I waited and looked over the parapet that when my turn came I would hop out quick like and take a zigzag course for the wood; but, believe me or not as you wish, all my scheming was wasted as old Fritz did not fire one round at another chap and I who were doing 600 yards in about 20 seconds more or less. To this day I can only put it down to the machine gun jamming just then, or perhaps [perhaps I say] Fritz recognised me as one he had fired at before when I was running up the chalk and he may have thought I was a ghost, as he did not know if he had killed me or not when I dived for cover into the trench head first. Anyhow chummy and I got back to the wood in one lump, and Fritz still did not fire, so as there were only a few more left to come they all spread out and bolted back together.

Now for the worst part of all. Everyone reached the wood safe and it's now Sunday morning so we set about making some breakfast. We were all busy blowing up our fires to make the canteens boil, and laughing and joking at the way we had dished old Fritz, when without any warning, Fritz opened out on our brand new trench and flattened it out, and then started firing at us in the woods with big shells and did so for almost all day out of spite, ruining a very nice Sunday towards the end of September 1914, while you were having breakfast in bed, a nice cooked dinner, and an afternoon stroll in the park, and then back home for tea, bread and butter, cake and jam. Just try to imagine our little troop of the "Old Contemptibles" who were huddled up like rabbits all that Sunday being shelled with "Jack Johnsons", shrapnel, and machine gun bullets, unable to get out to make a drop of tea for breakfast let alone teatime, and biscuits for dinner [army ration]. Some time during the evening Fritz relented and we were able to sit at the entrance of our holes to make a little fire each to make a drop of tea, but only after the threat of our officer that if anyone made the least smoke he would make us all put our fires out, and to keep a fire from smoking you have to keep blowing not "walking". But I'll not forget that Sunday in a hurry.

After that little lot we had it fairly quiet for a few days but please don't think we got away scot-free because we didn't. Then we suddenly had orders that we were on the move again. Great excitement I'll tell you, as things were getting monotonous. The orders came round to us one day early in October that we were being relieved by some French troops, "Zouaves"[15]. We paraded on the track running through "our wood", as we named it, and marched around to Battalion HQ in the quarries. After waiting around for a while in the dark, we formed up with rest of the regiment which had been strengthened by reinforcements from England, and moved off down towards Bucy-Le-Long in the valley. It was pitch dark and we had orders to make no noise whatsoever; no talking, no smoking, no nothing etc; I almost said no breathing, but we breathed a bit before we finished [of course we made no noise stumbling along over fallen tree trunks and potholes in the dark and cursing every time!] Now when troops get orders like that on "active service" in the dead of night it naturally leads them to think they are in for a night attack. So, I tell you, there were heaps of "muddied oafs" and much grumbling and grousing about the way we had been dished with the yarn about being relieved, and then taking us on a night attack. Grumbling and swearing could be heard all up and down the column regardless of the orders "no talking". Every now and then some officer or maybe a Sergeant would say, "Stop talking", "Take that man's name", "I've got it Sir", "Take it again", and so on, till what with one and another "chiming in" and "chewing the mop" I think to myself it would have been much quieter if the order had been "Everybody talk at once". But "Tommies" are always like that, and "Tars" are just as bad, so don't laugh you "Jack Tars".

We got clear of the wood and village at last and set out across the valley to the bridge, which we had come over nearly a month before, and then we had a big surprise. After marching for an hour we fell in for the usual "10 minutes halt", and when we fell in we were told that we could <u>talk</u> and <u>smoke</u>; talk and smoke whilst on a night march. Now I've just told you that if you tell troops on the march to "shut up" they don't always "shut up", but if you tell 'em to "keep talking" they'll probably be dumb, and that's what we found on that cold night march from the river Aisne. Either they had used up all their subjects during the first hours silent march or else the sudden order to talk and smoke [at night mind] left them speechless, and we were almost a "phantom army" [like that Russian army that went through England during the war]. Perhaps we were too busy to talk and enjoy our fags too, as it was a cold night I know. I said, "enjoy" mind. I can taste some of those "gaspers" yet. "Three Witches","Roughriders", and a few more, ugh. Still a smoke was a smoke in those days, and when all us smokers [and who wasn't a smoker out there?] got our pipes and fags going, to look up and down the column was like looking at a long line of glow-worms bobbing along. And the smell for us coming from the different "brands" of smoking mixture of those in front, makes me think that perhaps that it was from that night march that the idea of "gas" warfare originated. I wonder!

We marched nine miles on that night, and then bivouacked for the remainder of that night, and next day October 7th. The second night was only about five or six miles and we camped again October 8th. The same procedure for October 9th only we had about 16 or 17 miles to do that time, and on October 10th we arrived at the town of Compiègne about 8pm, and slept in the goods yard of the station, and at about 4am on Sunday October 11th we entrained, destination unknown, and we came via Amiens and Boulogne to Calais and we were in Calais about 4pm on Sunday 11th. [That was the nearest we had been to England since we left. Thought we were coming home. What hopes!]

The move from Compiègne

We went on till we arrived in the town of St Omer[16], where we detrained and went to a village called Bleadecques where we stayed 24 hours and then rode on motor lorries to a little village near Cassel[17]. We had breakfast in a field there, and then moved on up to the town of Baillieu. The company went into some big stables there for the night, but my platoon was unlucky and was detailed for outpost duty as soon as we arrived. The same old Sergeant, Sergeant Todd was in charge of us, so he had orders to take his platoon to some crossroads and erect a barricade across the road to stop all cars proceeding either way and search them, as spies dressed in British uniform were reported to be "running spare" about the country in motor cars. We proceeded to these crossroads some distance out from town towards the direction of where we were informed Fritz was settled down, and on arrival we found a little house a few yards away from the corner fully furnished but uninhabited. [Fritz had been through Baillieu a couple of days previous mind you], so, of course we had to perform the usual "scrounge round". Our first job was to erect a barricade. This we did by pulling down the garden fence of the little house and putting it across the road on two tubs, and pulling an empty wagon across the other road. There's the barricade, and we used the house for those not actually on sentry go, and were told that we would have a dixie of tea and some rations sent out to us as soon as the transport brought it up. We are still waiting for that dixie of hot tea; that sounded alright, but plans sometime go astray "on service", and, as I said, it was night time so excuses could be easily made.

Suffice it to say when the column marched up the road the next morning they brought with them about half a "dixie" of cold tea, some bread and "marg", and some fat cold pig, and we had to drink the cold tea quick and fall in behind them and march off with them, stuffing the bread and "marg" and the cold pig into our haversacks for "future reference". We were told that some tea and rations had been sent to out to us overnight, but they couldn't find us, so they returned and saved it for the morning. We were not hungry though, and the reason was this [of course we swore to the others we hadn't had a bite at the time, but we told them this afterwards]. Well now I happened to be on sentry duty with a pal named Richmond who was a good bugler, and could speak French fairly well. And when dawn broke him and I were together leaning against the wagon waiting for any "Rolls Royces", or "Fords", or "Woolworths", if you like, to roll up, when I spotted a good sized farm about 400 or 500 yards away to our front. I said to Richmond "Richy boy, as soon as I'm relieved I'm going to visit that farm for some grub". He said "Right I'll come". When two more lads relieved us, "Richy" and I told the sergeant where we were going to do and what for, as we had not had any grub since that breakfast [about dinner time] in the field the day before; you bet we were hungry, and by the way, October nights are not very warm are they, especially if you are standing about waiting for "Tin Lizzies" and the dawn to come. Anyhow off Richmond and myself goes up to and across the rough field to this big farm. We arrived to find the house and part of it was surrounded by the usual outhouses and the yard itself was to be entered by a huge wooden gate nine or ten feet high. We could see through the bars. No one was in sight, so we gave the gate a good "rattle", and "Richy" yelled out "Monsieur". Then we saw a youngster, I suppose, about 10 or 12, run screaming across the yard into the house and slam the door. He had the "wind up" [remember reader Fritz was here yesterday and the day before, and that these people in the farm had cause to remember it as I'll show you later]. So as we were probably the first British troops he had seen, it was only natural that the poor kid was scared. Anyhow, the old farmer and I suppose his wife, and two younger girls, maybe his daughters, about 24 or 25 years old, and the little boy, came and stood in the door way. Richmond yelled out "Nous etes soldat Anglais", [we are British soldiers].

I told him to stop "cussing" but it appeared to please the old farmer and his family as they ran to the big gate swinging it wide open saying "Tres Bon, Monsieur, Tres bon, Outré, Outré", which lingo I have discovered since meant "Very good, sir, very good. Enter, Enter", or words to that effect. So they were evidently pleased to see us and the old boy showed his pleasure by patting our backs and putting his arms around our shoulders [I thought he was going to kiss me], as we walked across to the house with him. The poor little boy was laughing and crying in turns hanging onto my arms and kissing my dirty muddy hand. When we reached the door the wife and daughters were talking all at once in their own lingo, and of course we couldn't understand all of it, but, by what Richy picked out and told me, those two girls had been through it with Mr Fritz.

We were bidden enter, and we were shown around the farmhouse with a steaming basin of "café au lait", some bread and butter and half a dozen eggs. After that the old boy gave us some "tabac". I reckon we ate there about an hour, and after the meal we stood talking in the house. When I say "we", I mean my pal and the Froggies, as my share of the conversation was an occasional "Oui, Monsieur", or "Oui, Madame", and then I didn't know what they had said, so I may have answered wrongly as my French in those days was limited. So I'll say that while they were all talking together one of the young girls suddenly fell to the floor in a fit, and the other girl and the mother carried her away to her room. Then the old farmer told my pal of Fritz's share towards that girl on the day or so previous. If I could have seen Fritz just then I would have blazed away every round of ammunition I had on me into him. Well we guessed our sergeant would be looking for us, so after calming their fears and assuring them that Fritz would never visit the farm again, we set off back to the crossroads loaded up with a couple of big French round loaves about 12 inches across, some eggs, and a canteen of fresh butter for our mates. The old boy wouldn't ask us for a cent for it altho' we offered to give him all we had [about 2 francs between us]. They came to the gate and waved until we reached the crossroads. The column came up the road about 12.30pm, so if we had not scrounged a feast we should have had no meal till then. And that is how we lived in the early days of the war, by scrounging. By that I mean the "fighting troops" not the "Base Wallahs", although, of course, I am perfectly well aware that somebody had to be at the "Bases" to help us do our job, so please do not think that I'm trying to insult or slight any other branches.

The farm was quite close to the level crossing adjoining Nieppe[18] railway station, and on the other side of the road was a nice little "café" [that for the benefit of any reader who was out there]. We had a stay of two or three days at this farm and I learnt to speak a little bit more French at the "little café at the corner". I was on guard at Nieppe Station on October 18th. While there I shot a big black dog, which went for me during the night. Also, on that guard, the order was to allow no-one to come from the direction of Fritz back through our lines, as spies were supposed to be everywhere at that time. While I was on, a party of women with a young chap about 18 or 19 came toward the gates of the level crossing, which were open. I went towards them and held my rifle across the opening with bayonet fixed, of course, and they all started jabbering together so I called the sergeant to come and sort it out. After a devil of a "How-de-do" I was given to understand that this youngster was the brother of the girl at the "café" at the corner who had run away and hid when Fritz was about a few days before, on account of Fritz taking all the youths of fighting age prisoners. So I took him to his sister and got in her good books at once [and that's how I learned a little bit more of the French language]. I enjoyed my little stay at Nieppe short as it was. Early in the morning of the 19th October we were moved to a field where we remained all day awaiting orders I guess, and on the night of the 19th October we slept in some sort of factory. Then on the morning of the 20th we got on the move and got to Armentières where we had to hang out a bit. I remember us going to a straw-rick near Armentières Station and getting straw to make a bed on the platform. On the night of the 20th we slept on the platform of Armentieres Station. On the morning of the 21st we had orders to go about 3 or 4 miles to our left front to drive out the enemy who had re-crossed the river. Easy to say but hard to carry it out.

CHAPTER **7**

Flanders

Plans must have come unstuck, as we crossed the frontier into Belgium and went into a little school where we were billeted for the night of the 21st October. The early morning of the 22nd found us on the move to carry out this "driving back business". We hovered about some roads, fields and woods for a good time, sparring for an opening at Fritz and awaiting for the cavalry scouts reports as to where he was, how strong he was, and such like. Then we moved up through a small wood, the trees of which were nut trees [I should say it was a wood for pheasants and such game as we came up against some wire netting on the far side]. When we got to the edge of the wood we were told to lie down and keep low. Coming through the wood in extended order we had passed some dead cavalry horses and some dead and wounded troopers, and had a few shells drop amongst us with various kinds of luck. While we lay at the edge of the wood waiting orders we were treated to several bursts of Fritz's machine gun fire all along our line. The bullets zipped into the branches and trunks of the trees all around us. The biggest trunk round was no bigger than a mans arm, and 'twas darned hard to have to lay there getting sprayed with bullets and not being able to see where they were coming from, as Fritz was firing from somewhere on the flank all through the trees and we had to lay there, till the chaps on our right either killed that gun crew or captured the gun. It was captured in the end after we had endured about half an hour's hair raising and cold-blooded feeling. I might say that if old Fritz had kept that gun just a little lower he would have hit every one in turn.

Now we were able to get up on our knees and look around, and I'll describe a picture for you of what I saw now. Looking through the wire netting we saw a field about 400 yards wide in front of us. On the right

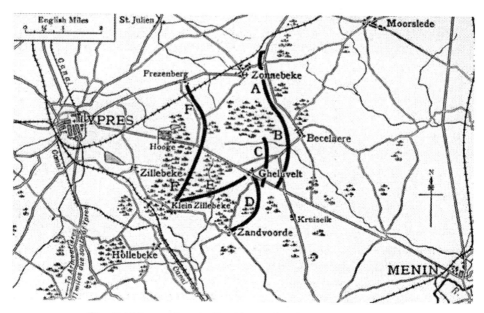

The British positions before Ypres, October 29–31st 1914

was a row of 6 to 8 cottages, and a road running in front of them. On the left was stonewalling running parallel with the cottages and at right angles with our wood. Scouts report that Fritz is holding the cottages, so to break down the wire netting and try to advance across that field to take the cottages would simply be "committing suicide". About 100 yards along the high stonewall on our left was a hole big enough to drive a lorry through, which Fritz had punctured with one of his "specials". Our orders were to take these cottages. Right. We moved off to our left in Indian file till we came to where the high wall touched the wood. There the wire netting was broken down and over we went creeping along under the wall till we came to the big hole. After the first two or three had nipped past the hole Fritz turned another darned machine gun on the opening and the rest of us had to duck to it. When we were all past we carried along the wall right to the end of it. Then we got into the open and crawled and wriggled our way along the furrows of the ploughed up field towards a hedge away to the left of the cottages, keeping Fritz busy by sniping at him from the trees and ditches, our job was to charge him from the left. We formed up under the hedge to get a good breath as we had a couple of hundred yards charge from there to the cottages in a minute. The order

British troops coming up towards Ypres late summer 1914

"Fix bayonets" was given us. Trembling with excitement, hats pulled well down, owing Fritz a lot of grudges for our dead pals, we stood there till the sergeant decided that everyone was absolutely ready for the final dash. While waiting there I well remember some of the remarks which were flying around. They went something like this, "Gawd blimey, wait till I meet that machine gunner who was "pasting us" in the woods just now", and another, "Wait till I get at those cottages, I'll have my own back for having to chuck in a good job in Blighty to come out here". All such talk as that was going on during that ten minute or so wait. Then all of a sudden "ready boys, charge". We burst through the openings of that hedge and across that couple of hundred yards of open field with a speed that would have left Applegarth, Shrubb, and even Nurmi, the crack runners, standing still. Yelling and shouting, stumbling and cursing Fritz, bayonets flashing, a couple firing as they run, we were over there before Fritz was aware of us, into the garden bursting open the doors of the cottages and up the stairs we dashed but Fritz's heart failed him. He didn't fight. As we

Entrance to Ypres from the Menin Road before the war.
The Menin Gate is now at the town end of the bridge

dashed over Fritz dashed out through the backs of the cottages, but they were not all quick enough. Just us little lot who charged the cottages captured 80 and killed many more. Some were in the parlours with their "hands up", some upstairs the same, as we dashed up. We fired from the bedroom window and back doors at those bolting across the fields at the back, and I remember especially getting one as he scrambled over the rear fence. When I shot him he was left hanging by his jackboot hitched at the top of the fence as he fell backwards. It was a proper scramble while it lasted, and we had orders not to chase them beyond the cottages, as it was getting towards the late afternoon by the time we cleared them all up. The ground at the back of the cottages was littered with dead and some crawling wounded, so we ceased fire. Our own commanding officer told us that that little scrap had been the means of Fritz losing 400 in killed and captured.

When things cooled down we were told we must hold these cottages in case of a counter-attack, and, knowing that Fritz would put his big guns on to the cottages as soon as he found out his infantry had lost them, we had orders to occupy a trench that Fritz had dug which ran across from the left of the cottages to the very hedge we had charged from behind, and had we only known it, we could have come up the hedge and jumped into the trench without having that mad rush across the open. But perhaps it was all for the best as we may have been spotted from somewhere else, and, anyway, we had done the job we were sent to do. Of course it had not been a picnic for us as we had lost some men since we started out in the morning, only, somehow, on a job like that you did not get a chance to know much about your own mates casualties until it was all over, as you had no time for any enquiries, you had as much as you could do to get on with the job of killing the other sides troops.

Well now, as I said, it's getting late and we occupied Fritz's trench. We kept a good look out and somebody started a bit of sniping. From where this chap was in the trench he could see a Fritz crawling across the field out in front on his hands and knees and, of course, was perfectly entitled to shoot him. Now if you remember I told you some time ago that a pal of mine had looted a pair of field glasses on the retreat from Mons, and that they were the means of saving a Fritz from getting shot. Well this is the Fritz. From where I was in the trench, I could see nothing, so when the firing started first by one, and then another, having a pop, I took my pal's glasses as I was wanting to see what the row was all about, being a "nosey parker". Those who were firing saw me with the glasses and one said "Bring those glasses here kidder" [Good old Totterdown – a part of Bristol]. Kidder did so, and by their aid I could plainly see that they were firing at a wounded Fritz. I could see that he was dragging his legs behind him, and now and then he would raise his arm to stop our lads firing. He had evidently been wounded by our fire from the cottages and had just recovered enough to crawl away, and our lads naturally thought that he was crawling up to have a snipe at us. I told our lads not to shoot any more, or he would have certainly been killed, as a couple more were considering having a pop at him. So that was one soul I saved that day[kind, ain't I?]. The other was a canary I liberated from a cage in the cottages, as the Belgians had fled leaving everything as it stood in that house, and Fritz had made a fine old mess in there.

Now let me tell you a little yarn I heard. It may be true or it may not, but it could easily have happened, as no one knew in those days where Fritz really was; we had not yet come to the trench warfare stage, so I'll let you hear it just as I heard it. After our little victory that day we were relieved by our other two companies and as we marched back in single file in the dark, I can see "Col Prowse", as I believe he was now, standing under a tree saying such things as "Good lads", and "Well done my boys"; that was the sort of man he was. Well, we came back to a barn for a nights sleep, and after a battle or skirmish like that there was always a hunt round to see how many of your old pals had gone to "Blighty" wounded, or "gone west", and, of course, different experiences had to be related. Among the yarns buzzing around that night was this one – it appears that the Quartermaster Sgt of the Enniskillen Fusiliers had lost his way in the darkness the night before on his way up with the rations and ammunition parties, and had been captured by Fritz, and that the other company of ours that fought on the right, while we had a go at the left, had arrived just in time to save some of the "Skins" from being captured also, as they were without ammunition and Fritz was attacking them when we "butted in". How far it was true I can't say, but it was quite possible as we were fairly well mixed up all over the place. Our CO was supposed to have given out the news that taking the day's fighting all through, it was estimated that 1200 had been killed, wounded or captured in our sector, and the prisoners "our little gang" captured in the cottages came from three different regiments with some Prussian Guards among them. I remember before the war reading an article in a book called the *Penny Magazine*, where it said the Prussian Guard were recognised as the "Terror of Europe". They were, perhaps, in peacetime but in war they held no terror for the Old Contemptibles.

Well now, we slept in that barn on the night of the 22nd and on the morning of the 23rd October we moved back and took up positions near some siege guns, and got nicely shelled for doing so. At night we moved up again to relieve the "Hants" who told us they had been there for two days. They were in some newly dug trenches.

They were more "holes in the ground" than trenches, as they had nothing to keep the sides up and the weather was none to kind to us about now. One good storm of rain and a blinking trench falls in. Let me tell you that just at this time we had no proper trenches like those who followed in later years. It was just a trench dug across a field, wood or road, with the front scooped out at intervals to enable one to sit upright in to sleep. No "duck board" tracks and "dugouts" with a flight of a thousand steps leading down into the bowels of the earth, and our barbed wire entanglements consisted of empty milk tins and, I believe, tins hung up on strings about a foot from

Somerset Light Infantry trenches near Ypres in Autumn 1914

the ground for Fritz to fall over and make a noise if he got an idea in his fathead to pay us a visit.

Well, as I have said, we came into these trenches, and before we had properly settled down, Fritz attacked us on our right. Twice during the night he came over and was driven back, and altho' he didn't come into the little bit of trench where our platoon was, we could see shadowy forms moving across out in front, and we let them have it, so that may have been the cause of his turning away. Our hole in the ground was only about 200 yards long, with no outlet either end, and then another trench 100 yards to our right or left with some more troops holding it. Had Fritz made a determined attack on any of these little positions he would have been bound to come in as we had no chance to get away, and we used to blaze away to our front at any old time there was a "war on" out there. There, at that time, we received the news that a general enemy advance was expected all along the line and to keep a good look out. We needed no warning, believe me, as we knew at this time what we had to deal with. An officer was shot in the leg and got away at night. Lance Corporal Russell was killed about this time. They say he was shot by a sniper clean through the head as he was peering over the parapet. I tell you we did not show our noses. The lads in reserve brought in rations at night. I did not envy them their job, bad as ours was.

The big advance did not take place, or I may not have been writing this.

Now we have worked our way up to Sunday 25th October. Nothing very special happened during the day except for continual sniping up and down the line, which made it rather "unhealthy", as the old trench was showing signs of wear and tear and we had no sand bags to repair it. On Sunday night as you were probably going to Church, reader, or "off out" to meet her, it rained in torrents which made it the most miserable night I had spent since the war started as regards the weather. The one consolation we got, if it can be called such, was the knowledge that our good old pal Fritz was getting it also.

The sides of the trench kept sliding in, we were up to our thighs in yellow slimy mud and water, we were soaked to the skin, cold and tired, and every other darned thing imaginable, and on top of that, as true as I write it, Fritz attacked, but for some reason or other we have never worked out, the attack "fizzled out", and we were left to our misery. I remember that night very well because a remark one of our mates made. He said, when the attack died out, "Blimey, why didn't Fritz come over and put me out of my misery?"

I expect that attack stopped owing to the fact that Fritz's rifles were the same as ours, too darned wet and full of mud to shoot with, and if he had come to our bit of trench we could only have jumped about in the mud to try and get unstuck.

I honestly believe that each one of us would have died that night to put us out of our misery. Well, the longest night has an end, and, by the way, that night seemed like a week to us, and we were very glad to see dawn breaking [though few of us can have expected it].

Which brings us to Monday 26th October. Fritz behaved like a little gentleman. He did not shell us till the early afternoon and then he set fire to a church in some town on our left. As night fell we could see a mass of flames coming from the tower. But the infantry and machine gunners were quiet as mice so we knew they had been drowned out during the night like ourselves and were busy repairing the trenches. When we saw ours in daylight it nearly made us weep. [I suppose soldiers are allowed to weep.] If we wanted to go a few yards to our right or left we had to climb up the muddy, slimy earth and then nip over. This game was soon stopped by Fritz letting us know he could see us bobbing about, so we had to throw anything that was wanted from one hole into another, as the trench now was nothing but a string of big holes half full of muddy slime and us wading about in it, like a lot of greedy pigs in a pond of hogwash.

I was never in such a blinking mess in my life as I was in some parts of France and Belgium. We had little hopes of starting fires for a drop of tea that morning, as everything was soaked, and our meals that day was cold-water, muddy bread and "marg", and some fat cold pig again. We sat in mud, slept in mud and drank mud from then until we were relieved on the Wednesday night. A chap in one of the other trenches near us bled to death, I was told, by getting a bullet in his leg that tore his vein so bad that it was impossible to stop the bleeding. Mind you, no help could come to us, nor could we go for help during daylight, and anyone who left their holes was "asking for it", and got it, from Fritz. So we just stayed in the mud waiting for anything to turn up, and if Fritz had sent over only a couple of well-directed "Jack Johnsons", he would have wiped us out, and I don't think anyone would have cared much if he had just then. We were past caring a damn what happened.

Tuesday night came and some rations and rum arrived, also the good news that we were being relieved tomorrow night [Wednesday]. By crumbs, we nearly wept with joy. All day Wednesday was used up by sniping at Fritz at any and every opportunity, and Fritz sniping at us, as we did not want to have too much to carry back at night, and that was the best way to get rid of ammunition. I forgot to mention that a new officer came to our trench to replace the one who got shot. This new one arrived on the Tuesday night and he was so blinking "windy" that he kept us "standing to arms" nearly all night. He cooled down when dawn broke which was lucky for him, because after the week we had just had we were "evil enough" to do "anything". Wednesday night came at last and some time during the dark hours we heard "bad language" and grousing coming from behind us and saw shadowy forms sliding and slipping about in the mud. [We knew it could not be Fritz got round the back of us by the "bad language" being used. Fritz couldn't have sworn in English like that.]

As they came up to the "trench" we were told to climb out and move off back. The Lord only knows what that regiment, the Hants, thought of that trench when they saw it in daylight next day. We felt sorry for them but more sorry for ourselves. We had spent nearly a week in that darned strip of mud, and we were glad to get out of it.

WITH OUR ARMY AT THE FRONT.
An officer's bomb-proof shelter, strongly built up with sand bags and branches.

A rather optimistic comment about the ruggedness of the shelter!

But the photo below shows some improvement by the winter

Number 1 breastwork, Ploegsteert Wood, winter 1914

We went back nearly a mile but were told that such was the shortage of troops, that we should have to be ready to go up again at any minute if Fritz made the big attack that was expected daily. We were bunged into a big stable with plenty of straw and hay about so we were able to wipe off some of the slime and mud, but were not allowed to take our boots off. I don't know that any of us wanted to take them off, particularly as we had no more clean socks or boots or puttees to put on, and it isn't very nice putting the muddy stuff back on again, is it?

Still we had a big fire there, and good hot food and rum rations and "fags", so that was some compensation, and we were all of us as merry and bright as it was possible to be under the circumstances.

We are now into the morning of the 29th October and our luck was in, as Fritz did not attack during the night. That day we had a complete change of underclothes given to us at last, shorts, pants and socks, but we had no clean khaki and putties, so that in a day or so we were all "crawling again". Still, we were able to get a wash and shave, which we, needless to say, wanted badly. Also we had a good sound sleep and another couple of good feeds that day. So on we go through a quiet Thursday followed by a quiet night, but on the 30th Fritz started first with shrapnel over the farm, and continued on and off all day. Plenty of hot bits of shell fell on the farmyard as we stood in the doorway, hearing the bits "fizz" as they dropped into little pools of water. About midday he started dropping "Jack Johnsons" and "Coal-boxes"[19] at the farm, and we had orders to move at a minute's notice. By the way, we had that order a few million times during the first weeks of the war! Well very soon after receiving that order this time, Fritz put a couple of beauties into the out houses of "our farm", and I think he got some of our lads. The remainder of us were ordered to clear out with all possible speed, and move to some trenches, which had been dug while we were spending that week in those mud-holes up in front. We did so, and from there watched Fritz wipe out our latest farm from the map of Belgium. The shelling continued all the rest of the day on Friday, and spread all along the front.

The Staff were buzzing around in great excitement, and the rumour reached us that this bombardment was to prepare the way for Fritz's big attack. [I believe it's history now that the first battle for Ypres began on Saturday October 31st 1914.] We had the usual order, "ready to move", and just after dark on Friday night we were ordered up to the mud-holes as Fritz was shelling them like blazes, to attack them. So we were in for a warm reception going up there through the barrage of shellfire, [it was not called a barrage then]. We started out but I never reached there. [I reached Deaconess Hospital, Edinburgh, instead.]

We were going up the lane towards the farm that Fritz had shelled us out of during the day, and wondered if we would live to see tomorrow's sunrise, when Corporal Chidgey who was our platoon corporal was taken

ill with ague. He shook like a leaf, and Sergeant Todd told me to take him
back to the first aid post and then come on up and find them again. I asked
the Sgt where he thought they were going but he had no idea. So he
simply said, "If we are gone from here, we'll be up in the front somewhere
and you'll find us sooner or later". Some instructions, that, but he knew I
was a good scout and scrounger [ahem]. Now if anyone who reads this
diary has ever had the luck, good or bad, to be roaming about in a strange
country, all alone for the greater part of a cold October night, with shells
flying about everywhere and bullets whizzing in all directions, they will
have some idea of how I spent the time trying to find my company. I took
the Corporal's arm around my neck, and carrying his gun and my own, we
set off back to find the first aid post. He was a heavy man and had little use
in his legs, so I soon began to sweat. Moreover, I hadn't the slightest idea
how far I would have to go to find the first aid post. We passed several lots
of troops going up into action so I guessed that something big was
expected. I yelled at one lot and asked them for the nearest MO, and was
told that there was one about half a mile away down on the main Menin
Way in a wood. [How did I know where the Menin Road was then? He
might just as well have said the Taku Road, China, for all I knew where
the Menin Road was.] Still I tracked on with my load of Corporal and
came to a main road set with cobblestones, where some transport wagons
were halted, and enquired again. I was told, "just down the road in a
wood", so I went just down the road and found it. I handed over the
Corporal and set back off.

And from there my troubles really started, and I had a nightmare night. I
found the track alright where my company had gone up, and which started
off up that way, but as I drew near the place I thought I had left them, I
was cheered up by Fritz dropping a salvo of "coal boxes" just on the track
ahead of me. I waited to see if there were any more to come, and there
was, and some more. I thought, "This is lively" so what is the next move?
As Fritz seemed to be spiteful about something just there, I decided
amongst myself to leave that track and go off to my left across country, as
there was a big hedge on the right. I made a big half circle and tried to find
the track beyond the shellfire as by experience I knew that the shells were
big stuff by the explosions. Old Fritz seemed determined that no transport
or reinforcements should come up that track, for a bit anyway.

Off I goes to the left, tracking my way through the mud of "sunny

Belgium", in the middle of the night, trying hard to think of anything but the war [to keep my pecker up, I admit], but old Fritz kept reminding me with those darned shells. As long as he kept them there I didn't mind, but you never knew out there what Fritz was going to do next. I could hear a devil of a "strafing" going up in front, and as I worked my way up to the frontline trenches, falling in shell holes full of water, over fallen tree trunks, and past a dead cow or horse, stumbling and swearing I was, believe me, I gradually fell nearer the range of spent bullets which were moaning their way across. I came round towards the track when I thought I was far enough up to miss those shells, and I at last found a track just near a forked road. Now I wondered which one to take. There was not a soul in sight, but I heard voices a little way up the right hand one so I was on it like a bird. About 50 yards from the fork in the road I found a machine gun crew in reserve of my own regiment. Sgt Dagger was in charge [he was sadly killed at the end of November 1914], and I knew him well as we were school kids together. I said, "Joe, have you seen my company go up this track?" but he told me that no troops had been up this track for at least an hour. So I begged a swig of tea as they had a bit of a brazier going and had made some tea. He also said that he heard some troops going up the road to the left, but who they were he didn't know. So after a little chat I went back to the fork, and went up the left one to try my luck. I hadn't gone far when I met some stretcher bearers carrying back some wounded. I asked them how things were looking, and one of them, a jock by his talk, said "Mon it's awful, you won't go far on that road". We all stayed talking a little while and amongst the other things they told me was that Fritz was spraying the track a little further up with machine gun bullets in an almost continuous stream. I had heard a pretty constant fire by a machine gun all the way up from the fork but didn't know that's where he's putting it, so I was glad of the tip off, although I would soon have found out where he was putting 'em as I got up there.

One good tip deserves another so I was able to give them the tip where the shells were dropping down the track, and told them the way I had come, but it's one thing for a man to go across country in the dark with the ground full of shell holes, and quite another matter for two men to carry a wounded chum on a stretcher over the same ground. However after they had gone and I was left on my own again, I went on up the road as I had quite enough tracking and falling in to shell holes half full of water, some with bloated, stinking, dead cattle in them. I was pulled up short by a sudden burst of bullets from the machine gun the stretcher-bearers had told me of. I threw myself flying into the ditch at the roadside and waited for him to stop it. I think I said a few prayers while I crouched in that muddy ditch. They stopped at last and I jumped up and bolted up the road. Anyhow I was passed that now, thought I. There was a good scrap going on up in front as I could tell by the shell bursts and the machine gun and rifle fire, and I was getting plenty of spare bullets flying around me by this time. Also I confess I was getting "windy" out there mooching around on my own in the dark. I could not make out any special place to go to find my company, and little further up the road I spotted a newly shell shocked tree. I guessed it had been newly fetched down by the smell of the chemicals of the shell that hit it, and as it was a good "thick un" I thought I'd have a rest by it till someone came along either way. I don't know how long I stopped there thinking, smoking and wondering, [wondering how long it would be before Fritz sent over another shell to start chopping up the tree he had felled, and me with it]. Presently some chaps of the Hampshire wounded started making their way back. Seeing me there they asked me how far it was to the first aid post. I reckoned it was about a mile, so we sat on the tree talking. They told me it was hot stuff up in front, and that I should have a very poor chance of finding my company. So I told them to nip to it when they got near the spot where the machine gun was spraying the road further down, and they went on back. They were all "walking cases" [that is, wounded but able to walk]. They had not gone far when that d——d machine gun started again, and they nipped back to the tree where I sat. They were "running cases", excuse the joke, as having been wounded once by Fritz they didn't want to risk another, so I said "I'll show you down as far as the fork road", as there did not seem much chance of finding my company that night, and then I would report to the machine gun Sergeant. So I went right back to the road where I met the transport over night, and told the wounded Hants where the first aid post was, and then went back up the fork road again. And we did not loiter going past those two places where the machine gun played and where Fritz dropped the big shells, although he had stopped it now.

Well, after wandering around near all night, on my own, and in company, I reached the machine guns crew's dugout, and told the Sergeant just how things were and that I was going to stay here till daybreak and have another go then. They had some straw on the ground, and I sat down and told the chap on sentry that if I dozed off to "give us a kick just before dawn", but I had about an hours kip and just before dawn on October 31st I was out looking for my company again. I went up the right fork this time, and having learnt from experience that just before dawn was a good time for getting about I hurried along without meeting anyone. The country about here was pretty flat, but wooded, and I had no idea where Fritz could see me from. I came to a village that didn't have a sound wall standing and looked out into the surrounding country, and wandered about a bit till I heard a voice say "Come down you —— fool! Thees get your head shot off in a minute". I needed no second telling and jumped down in to the trench which was held by "C" Company of our regiment. The chap who had greeted me so politely was a pal of mine in peacetime, named Baker, commonly known as "Basher Baker". How was I to know I had been wandering around in "no-man's land"? It appears I back-worked my way through gaps of the different companies [easy enough to do], and was coming towards "C" company's trenches from the direction of Fritz's trenches when he saw me. No wonder I hadn't seen any troops knocking about. A Sergeant of this company came out of a hole in the side of the trench and seeing me there asked me which way I'd come; so I pointed out the way and he said I must be the luckiest bloke ever to be alive. He took me and Basher Baker about 50 yards along the trench and said "Look out there". I did so and I saw about 18 or 20 dead Fritz's just over the parapet, and a couple actually on the sand bags. The machine gun had caught them a treat, and the fellows there told me they could hear Fritzs scream as the bullets hit them. As I have mentioned already we had no barbed wire then, and Fritz had got very close that time before he was stopped.

I said to the Sergeant "Well I have been wandering about there for the last half hour or so and no-one has shot at me, so perhaps Fritz has gone back into those woods over there, and I want one of those Fritz helmets". He said I could please myself about that but I would have to stand the racket if Fritz started firing again. So saying that I would chance it, I climbed up the trench side followed later by Basher. We saw the Fritzs lying dead all around us in every possible shape it was possible for a man to twist himself into. I turned one over and some letters fell out of his valise strapped to his back, and as it may have been useful for identification purposes I stuffed them back in again. Two or three wore gold-rimmed eyeglasses. Then I saw a helmet I fancied and picked it off one of the heads. The chap must have been shot in the head, and as I was viewing the helmet with my left hand up inside, some of the congealed blood ran through my fingers. Somehow that turned me right off taking it and I threw it down and was looking round for another one. Fritz had obviously been watching our movements and seeing that we were not there attending to his chaps who may have been wounded over night, he started sniping at us, so Basher and your 'umble servant had to beat it without a helmet after all. Had I known I was going to be on my way to Edinburgh before the next day came I would have grabbed one and ran, but I thought I would have plenty of time to get one later on.

That was the worst of it out there, "You never can tell". Now while this little performance had been going on up the right track of the forked road, my company "B" Coy had gone away back by the left track, but I didn't know it, so when I got back down into the trench and had been right choked off by the Sergeant, I asked him if he had any idea where "B"Coy was as I had been searching all night for them. He could only say they were over on the left somewhere, so leaving them to get on with the war I came back on this side of the ruined village and worked my way around till I met some of the Hants. They informed me that some of our lads had gone back a couple of hours ago, so they must have gone down the left track about dawn as I was going up the right track also at dawn, which goes to show that I was a good scout by saying that just before dawn was a good time to get about the country [ahem].

Any old how I had to track all the way back as no-one was willing to adopt me, and between you and me I was not that anxious to get adopted up there, after that week in the mud-holes, and my night out, so off I went right back to the main Menin Road where I had taken the sick Corporal overnight, and found them in a field. So I had a nice little jaunt.

Fritz was very kind to me all the way back, but I well remember the creepy feeling when I was near the spot where the machine gun played on the road, also when I was passing the shell holes further back. I admit to you that I did not hang about viewing the country. Well, I found my company in the field about 9am Saturday October 31st, and was greeted with these words "Here thee bist reported missing believed killed". So I answered, "Well before thee's bury I, gie's some breakfast". [We were not very particular about our speech out there you see.] They had had a "roll

Temporary Somerset graves near Ypres

call" and mail had arrived from England that morn, and the letters for me had been sent back stamped saying "Missing. Unable to trace" [which accounted for the fact of my people at home receiving returned letters stamped with that on, and, of course, getting the "wind up" thinking your 'umble had been taken prisoner or "gone west"]. My pals had thought that as I had taken the sick corporal back overnight, and had to come on up the track behind them, that I had met those shells which Fritz dropped over as they had heard them dropping behind them. But I had luckily made the half circle around them. One comic said "We looked for the bits when we passed the place coming back this morning, but couldn't see none". There was always plenty of chaff flying about like that when the danger was over [for the time being], so I tucked into breakfast and let them get on with it. I remember cussing a bit though because my letters had been sent back to transport, and there was little chance of getting them. Neither did I, as they went back to England again.

We were told we should stay where we were for a little while, and some time during the morning a load of underclothes came up from transport, the second lot since England in August. Fags and things were served out, and we promptly started changing there in the field. [I'm telling you this for a reason.] This field was alongside of what I had been told was the Menin Road. Along each side of the road were high trees, and a small hedge ran around the field, and in one corner stood a little house occupied by an elderly woman, and there were a couple of sheds near the house. Now reader, have you got all that? Right! Now when we had changed our shirts, pants, socks etc, we hung the dirty stuff on the little hedge and spread it out on the grass to air a bit. [And to kill a few of our <u>bed chums</u> which we all had.] That was all very nice, and the field soon began to look like a draper's shop during the "rummage sale", and everyone seemed to overlook the fact that the one above sees all. By that I mean that Fritz had a string of observation balloons [called German sausages by us] up in the air behind his trenches. But no one seemed to worry as they said such things as "He can't see us all back there, and if he could he would not object to a few blokes changing their lousy shirts." But it seems Fritz could see us and did object. Perhaps he was jealous of our clean shirts Anyhow, a few big'uns came over and hit mother earth with a crash some distance over the road to our left facing Fritz. One or more had landed smack into a farm which we knew for certain was A Company's HQ for the time being. I saw a big cloud of dust from the red tiles go up into the air. God knows how many were killed in that first salvo. Of course Fritz was able to get the exact range of the road as he only had to refer to a map and he had it, as we were all practically on the main road from Menin to Ploegsteert [nick-named Plug street]. Plug street wood was on the right edge of the field we were in. Evidently Fritz used a map for it was wonderful shooting, and in about 29 minutes a second salvo came over and fetched down a tree like a knife cutting a banana. And they were big trees too! We had been hanging about the field nearly all day awaiting orders, and dozing and trying to clean ourselves up a bit in case of a move up the line again. One or two more salvos came over at intervals, and it seemed that each time they were getting closer to our field. So orders were given out to get our straps on and be ready "to move away any minute". Fritz must have thought that those salvos were enough to be going on with as he stopped firing for a bit, so we were told to get a meal while we had a chance and to keep our straps on and rifles handy, ready to grab if he started again.

A pal and myself decided to make a canteen of tea. We got 4 bricks and collected some bits of wood and soon we had a little fire going by the wall of the shed belonging to the little house. The shed itself was right under the over-hanging branches of the big trees on the road. It was late in the afternoon of October 31st so it would soon be dark. We had our little fire going and two canteens full of water on the fire, but that tea was never made. Fritz started shelling again, and I was on my knees blowing the fire up to make it burn up quick, and my pal was "keeping styke" to tell me how far the shells were dropping away, and every now and then he would jump down from the house and say "Hurry up kid, he's getting nearer".

But the darned canteens wouldn't boil. All of a sudden there was the most deafening crash I've ever heard in my life. I had heard no shell coming, only this murderous crash. I felt myself blown sprawling along the ground, pieces of stones and tiles were falling on me and a long piece of sheeting fell across my arm as I lay there wondering if the end of the world had come. I was able to see and think but I was unable to move or hear. I struggled to rise but couldn't and all was very peaceful and quiet. Then I heard a voice which seemed to come from the clouds say "Come on kid, run!" Suddenly all my feelings seemed to come back with a rush and I jumped up and I grabbed my gun ready to shoot each and everyone.

I felt just as I imagined a madman would feel. My eyes were smarting and burning and full of tears. There was a singing noise in my ears and my head was buzzing like a thousand bees. I bolted towards the voice and as I ran I saw little puffs from shrapnel shells in the air around me. But if all the shrapnel that Fritz had was bursting over me at once I don't believe I would have been hit then. After that terrific bang the bursting of shrapnel shells sounded like popguns. As I flew over the ground I saw an officer and two of our chaps dashing along ahead of us for the woods [Plugstreet wood], and when I caught up with them in the wood, the officer was sprawling on the ground vomiting enough to bring two hearts up, and the two lads laying down beneath him were gasping for breath. I could see no other troops about and could hear nothing, so I just flopped down alongside them and felt as though I should like to die, or sleep for a year. How long we lay there I don't know, but some time or other I was awakened by one of the other chaps and he said, as I sat up, that he believed the officer was dead. I crawled to him and pulled him over on his back and then I thought he really was dead. He was a sight. His eyes were staring wide open, and his face, although deathly pale seemed greyish green in the night-light. I said to the two chaps "We'd better get him away somewhere", and we dragged him to his feet somehow and started off in a bunch through the woods with no idea where to go. We eventually arrived at what seemed to be a gamekeeper's house, and one of the others banged on the door and it was opened by an old Belgium woman. We all four went in and laid the officer on the bed inside, and took his straps off. We could not speak "Belge", of course, so we decided amongst ourselves for the other two to go for help, and I was to stay with him. I could do nothing for him, so I gave him a drink from his water bottle, which he promptly fetched up again. I had a swig and I was sick then. The funny

Lt Prideaux

part about the job was that altho' I had lost my grub and tea, I did not feel
a bit hungry or thirsty; I only wanted to sleep forever. All my haversack
rations were gone as I had laid them out on the ground ready for a meal
when the big bang came.

After a while the other two chaps came back and said they had found some
transport lines where they could take him. So off we go again with an arm
each around our necks and the other carrying his straps, to where they
thought the transport was, but we lost our way in the dark wood, and
found a battery of heavy guns instead. We enquired from the gunners and
were directed, and almost as soon as we left the battery Fritz dropped some
shells amongst them. We went on as fast as we were able to go, but it's no
joke when you are dead beat and lugging a man along, with no use in him
and very little use in yourself, altho' at this time I was hearing more now,
but felt as wobbly as a chicken. We at last arrived at the edge of the wood
on to a road, and saw some lights of houses up the road. One direction
being as good as another, we went towards them and one was an estaminet
[café].

The other two lads went to buy or beg a drink, but I did not feel like
eating, drinking or smoking anything, I sat at the roadside with the officer
lying in a heap on the bank. As I sat there I saw someone coming up the
track with a horse, and when he got near enough I asked "Who's that?"
and found it was our transport officer Lieutenant Prideaux [lilled in
January 1917], on his way up with the ration wagons.

He asked about the trouble and I explained the whole situation to him as
far as I was able. So he asked me if I was alone seeing that I had three rifles
and I had to say that two more had gone "in there" to get some coffee.
When they came out he made them go with him on the wagons, and told
me to stick with the officer till I came to the first aid post.

I suppose he made them go with him because he had found them in a café. They helped me get the officer to his feet and hanging his straps round my neck like a bridle, I was off down the road again. My crumbs it was hard work as he was not a lightweight by any means. He had not spoken a word all the way through and for all I knew another shell may have got him when I had mine, and perhaps he was dumb. Now I was all alone on that cart track with about 14 stone of half dead officer hanging across my neck. Well I don't suppose even Samson himself could have stuck that for long if he was feeling in the same condition that I was then; so after struggling along for a few minutes I felt him slipping lower and lower and as I couldn't hold him, I let go and he fell down flop in the dirt and I fell down beside him. I don't know how long we remained there but I was aroused by a Red Cross car without lights nearly running over us. I yelled for help and an officer of the RAMC who was sitting beside the driver got down to see what it was all about. Once more I explained and he had a stretcher brought out and the officer was put on it and was placed in the car.

CHAPTER 8

Hospital Ship
and Train to Edinburgh

I have no clear recollection of what happened after that, and I cannot explain how I found myself in a hospital train all covered in blankets. But as near as I can remember I'll try to describe my feelings while I was talking to the officer of the RAMC. I lay on the dirt of the road while I was explaining the facts to him and as I was talking I seemed to be slipping down, down, down somewhere and the officer's voice seemed to be getting fainter and fainter, and I just remember them taking up the sick officer from the ground and then I knew no more till I woke up in broad daylight and found myself in a train going somewhere, and as I opened my eyes I heard a woman's voice saying "You look cold Tommy". I thought then "I'm in heaven and that's an angel". But it was a nurse standing by my berth in the train [Still, they were angels all the same to us lads out there]. I didn't answer her, I couldn't somehow, so I just smiled, and she went and fetched a mug of hot milk from somewhere. I tried to take it but I couldn't stop shaking so she held it for me to sip some. I asked her "Where are we?" but she said "You go to sleep and I'll wake you when we get to the boat". "Boat", I thought "am I off to Blighty?" I needed no second telling to go to sleep and dozed off again. When I was awakened we were at Boulogne and I was carried down to the dockside where I saw the hospital ship *Asturias*, and was taken aboard sometime, and we sailed in the dark.

Somewhere on the way up through England we had some rolls and butter given to us, and some tea, and I ate that although I had no taste for food. It was as near as I remember Monday when we reached Edinburgh, to find the station packed with people throwing flowers and sweets onto the ambulance cars as we drove through the streets to the hospital. I don't know what I looked like myself but you may guess when I tell you that I had on the same boots, khaki and puttees that I had done the Retreat from Mons in; so you will know what the heels and soles [mark that] were like. Also I still had some of the mud aboard me from that week in the "mud hole trench", and I hadn't washed or shaved since that Saturday morning. In my case that meant a beard like "Old Bill" in the "Better 'ole"[20]. Anyhow appearances counted for nothing with the people of Edinburgh and complete strangers who brought in cakes and fruits often visited us. One Scottish lady discovered that I was in the same regiment that her brother had been an officer in years ago, and she made a proper fuss of your 'umble. On arrival at the hospital I said I would try to walk from the ambulance up the stairs, into what looked like an infant school turned into a hospital. At least that's what I thought it was, as there were a lot of painted animals all around the walls of our ward like you would see in an infant school.

I found I could walk with the aid of the orderly's arm around my waist, so I entered Deaconess Hospital, Edinburgh. All particulars being taken we were given a good bath and had a shave, and I had a change of underclothes and real sheets. Our khaki was burnt so I was told later when I enquired for some photos and my fag case, but we still kept our boots, and later on when we were discharged from Hospital we wore them home. They were worn down flat at the heels and soles, which made me stare when I recently went to see the picture on the film of "Mons". I particularly noticed that all the heels of the troops' boots in the picture were up level which somewhat gave the game away. Anyhow after about a three weeks stay or maybe a month I was discharged with eight or nine others and we were served out with some second hand clothes which people had given to the hospital for the benefit of those discharged to reach their homes in. It appeared all khaki was wanted for troops going over there. I had a walk round Edinburgh with the others till we had to go to Waverly Road Station to catch our different trains, and I'm sure the people of Edinburgh must have thought we were a gang of Belgian refugees, in our comic second suits. We did look some guys.

All the lads who came from the hospital with me had to go to different parts of England, so at 6.30 pm I left Waverly Road Station, Edinburgh, and had a carriage to myself all the way to Fishponds, Bristol where I arrived about 7am next morning. I changed to a train there for Bath. I had a month's leave which just took me past Christmas, and I rejoined my depot early in January 1915. I stayed there about a week and got fitted out

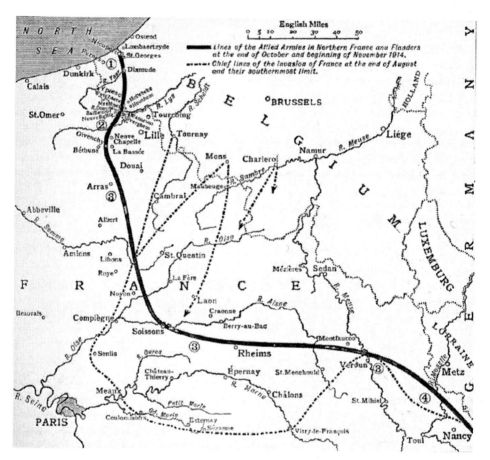

*Lines of the Allied Armies in Northern France at the end of October
and beginning of November 1914*

with khaki once again, and then off to old Plymouth. I went to the huts at
Crown Hill and after attending hospital for a little while I was once more
pronounced fit. I joined the signallers there and about the middle of April
I was sent out to France again, with a draft.

CHAPTER 9

Return to Ypres

I rejoined the regiment on the Yser Canal bank just near Ypres[21] in April 1915. What a difference in the trenches I left in October and those I was in now. Dugouts of a sort and deep trenches were everywhere, but even then old Fritz used to smash it up quite easily as by that time trench warfare had set in, and he had brought up plenty of big guns. I was in the front lines where the regiment was now and it was pretty free from big gun fire, as Fritz's front line and ours was so close together that had the big guns of either side shelled much they would most likely have killed their own troops. To give you some idea how close we were to Fritz I'll tell you that one night some of our troops were sent over on a raid. We heard that HQs wanted some information as to what troops of Fritz's army was holding the line in front and, as Fritz would not tell us if he had been asked in the ordinary way, the only way to find out was to go over and collect a few prisoners. Sounds simple doesn't it! Well, our lads went over and had a cut at Fritz and brought back some prisoners. Of course we had some killed and wounded in the process, and a couple of nights later after a small patrol went out to do a "bit of reconnoitring" and one man was sent back with a message. He did not arrive and in the morning Fritz called across to us to say they had caught him, and held up a letter with a stamp and all on it for us to see. So you can see how close our front line was to Fritz's front line to be able to see a stamped envelope.

I was now attached to Battalion's HQs as signaller, and one day a chum and myself were told to go off to go up around the trenches and repair or "peg up" any telephone cable that might be found broken. We had been crawling about following the cable up one trench and down another for a couple of hours, putting things straight, when I thought it was about time

𝕭𝖑𝖎𝖈𝖐 𝖆𝖚𝖋 𝔜𝖕𝖊𝖗𝖓

German view of Ypres from Hill 60, and showing the ruins of the Cathedral and the medieval Cloth Hall

to be getting back; being curious to know how things looked out in "No Man's Land", I climbed up the side of the trench to have a squint over the top, I remember seeing a big jack boot standing up out of a shell hole, but whether there was a leg inside I don't know, but I had just ducked my head to say to my chum, "Have a decks [look], over here", when a sniper who had evidently been watching me, fired, and a bullet went smash into the sandbag that my chin had been resting on. [Let me whisper this], I did not look over there again. My pal said "Thee's better get down", I answered, "Chummy I am down", as I fell down. Hundreds of little incidents like that occurred all through the war, with various kinds of luck, some good and some bad. If a person's luck was in, he might get away with a trip to the Base, or to England in hospital, and if his luck was out, he would not, and would reside permanently in France, in a soldier's grave. However that's what we had a shilling a day for, so let's get on with the story.

Things were more or less the same old routine day in day out, which was very monotonous, and I was very glad when one day the Signal Sergeant

View of Ypres today from the ridge near Paschendaele.
The rebuilt Cloth Hall dominates the skyline. A ridge only 200 feet high
gave a commanding advantage in the Ypres Salient.

said to me "It's your turn to go to Brigade's HQs, as orderly for a fortnight". So getting my straps and rifle together, and what bit of kit I possessed, I packed up and went back to the farm just behind the Yser canal, and reported to the Signal Sergeant there of the RE Signals. The job was to take all–important messages to Battalion HQ's and then back to transport lines, and any other places where needed. Also I was to guide any new troops or officers up to their respective regiments, which was a nice kind of way to find one's way about. I know I swore over having to leave my pals at Battalion's HQs at the time, but when my fortnight was up I had enjoyed myself so much that I hankered after staying for another fortnight. After a bit of palaver over the phone between the Battalion Signal Sgt and the Brigade Signal Sergeant it was arranged that the Brigade Signal Sgt could send me back to the regiment when he got fed up with me. This worked well in my favour, as the Signal Sergeant RE said that as long as I was in charge of the signal section, I should never go back to the regiment, as he had been looking for a good "visual flag waver" for a long time, and without wishing to boast I was considered "hot stuff" at flag wagging [not chin wagging]. However, to show you in passing just how I got on at the Brigade's HQs, suffice it to say that I

Strong points in the walls and ramparts of Ypres

never rejoined my regiment again during the whole war, becoming permanently attached to Brigade's HQs as orderly and spare operator, Ahem! That speaks for itself, and after a while I transferred to the RE Signal Corps, now was I happy.

I soon chummed up with my new pals [a habit I've got], and when I got used to the run of things, I could see I was on a good thing.

An outing with Brigadier-General Prowse

The General in charge was Brigadier General Prowse, my old Major from Mons, and as good a soldier that ever went across the Channel. I have walked many miles in the course of my duties as orderly with Brigadier Prowse, not behind him, as most officers make you walk, but alongside him, where the path or trench was wide enough to allow it, chatting with him, and sharing his "fags". He was the sort of General who made life worth living, and we lost a good pal when he was killed on the first morning of the Somme battle.

One day I well remember him coming out of the farmhouse and shouting "orderly", so I jumped to my feet to salute him. He said "Are you orderly today?" I said, "Yes sir". So he took me back into the room he had in that farmhouse, and showed me part of the trenches in our part of the line. "Sit there", he said "and study that". I did so. Now he said, "We, you and

I, are going to have a nice long walk all around here and here", pointing out on the map, and "It's going to take us all day" he continued. So telling me to get my rifle and bandolier of ammunition, some haversack rations, and a bottle of water, and to report to him in half an hour, he went off out of the room. I was ready when he called me again, and on a lovely day towards the end of June 1915, Brigadier Prowse and myself set out at about 9am. I was with him till sundown. And I will now try to tell you the happenings of the day. It appeared afterwards that he was having a personal inspection of the front line trenches, preparatory to an attack which was being made on some of Fritz's first line trenches on July 6th 1915, and he wanted some first hand information, and this was the way of getting it. As I say we started off preparing for anything, me walking alongside of him and smoking his "fags" [see final end note page], talking about the weather and England, about home life and peacetime soldiering, anything except the war, till we eventually arrived at the Yser Canal bank. It was rather hard to describe it, but for the benefit of anyone who may happen to read this, and "who were not there", I'll try to show you what my impression was of the Yser canal, Belgium. In peacetime I should have called it beautiful no doubt, but I only saw it in wartime. Peacetime scenery is kept for the "Jack Rich". Wartime scenery is for the "Hard-working Poor", meaning "Tommy" and "Jack", who then "sees the sights" at the Government's expense? [Or the taxpayer.] However the Canal in 1915 looked to me as though it had had a very bad attack of small pox [shell holes], and as though the trees which lined the banks had been nibbled by millions of rats, as big as elephants, torn, twisted, blown up, blown down, shelled day after day with all sizes of shells. It was a proper mess, in fact I used to think it would never be straightened till the end of the world came, and I don't suppose it will be properly. The troops had made holes in the banks to live like rats; 'twas" holes, as you could not call them dug-outs at least that's my opinion after seeing some of the German dugouts we captured. He knew how to build dugouts. We learnt from him later, but could never beat him at it [credit where credit's due]. Well now, the General and I got to the canal bank, and seeing a bunch of "Tommies" sitting outside their "rat holes", he stopped and had a chat with them, then on again along under the bank we went towards Ypres till we came to a wooden bridge which our troops had put across the canal. It looked a bit "moth-eaten" as Fritz had fired a few "moths" at it at different times, and it was pretty wobbly to walk over, so I remember thinking that I would not care to rush across there with a lot of troops or we should all be in the canal, which was a nice "slimy green". Nothing special happened till we arrived at the Right Battalion's HQ where the "Gen" went in to have a chat with the CO, and I sat in the trench and waited. Near about an hour later he came out and we studied the trench map together again, and he said "Now you take this map, and lead me to that point on the map". I did so and started off. Map reading comes easily to a trained signaller, Ahem. We reached the point indicated in about an hour, which was a Company HQs, not much more than 200 yard from the front line trench, we arrived without loss, but very hot and thirsty, so I suppose that accounts for the Brigadier spending a good hour in the dugout with the officers. It was nearly midday now and boiling hot in the June sun, so I had bread, bully and water for some dinner [and a "General's fag"]. Fritz's trenches were so close together just about here that there was very little shellfire from our artillery or Fritz's guns, as they were liable to kill their own troops, so as long as one kept his head down he was fairly safe. So I had dinner and a doze, sat in the trench. The General came out and asked for the map and said "Now I want you to lead me to this 'sap head' marked on the map." For the benefit of those not in the know I'll explain that a "sap head" isn't a "fat head", but a trench leading out from our front lines nearly into the enemy's line, and to get to those kind of places safely, one must NOT advertise the fact that he is about, as Fritz had a nasty habit of trying to stop you with a bullet. So we started off for the sap head, and I suppose we must have shown too much of "the whites of our eyes" or something, anyway Fritz let us know he was awake by sniping at us on the way up, without hitting us thank you. The General only said "Bad man, next week you will be sorry for that", which made me wonder what he meant, so I said casually "Why next week, Sir?" and he said, also casually, that we going to do a bit of "clearing up" over there next week as the snipers had got very troublesome and must be learnt better. That's how he put it. Later on I'll tell you of my little share in the attack, and also how I didn't get the DCM or MM, although I was told I earned one. And later again I'll show you how medals were dished out like rations at times so they were looked upon as rubbish, but that's another story.

Having reached the sap head "all the more together", as it were, the General just enquired how things were looking and had a little chat with Sgt in charge, and then we consulted our map, and he picked out another Battalion's HQs and said, "We'll go there". We went and arrived safe.

Parts of the old trenches,
Sanctuary Wood, Ypres

Now I have described this little days "outing" pretty fully just as a tribute to Brigadier General Prowse to let you see that he was one of the old school of soldiers who went with his men. I don't mean to say the New Army officers don't go where the men go into action, but Gen. Prowse was soldier and man combined and didn't treat a private soldier as a cannibal, as some Colonels whom I could name did. However we did at last arrive back at the farm sometime in the evening after a walk round the front line trenches for about 8 hours. It had been a great experience, with a few creepy feelings down the spine at intervals, and I was tired, so after a swill and tea I went to "bed" in the straw.

The Pilkhem Attack July 1915

Next day was my day off so I took a bike and rode back to Popereinghe. Fritz must have got to know somehow that I was visiting the town, as he shelled the railway station. Which was a compliment to my greatness, I

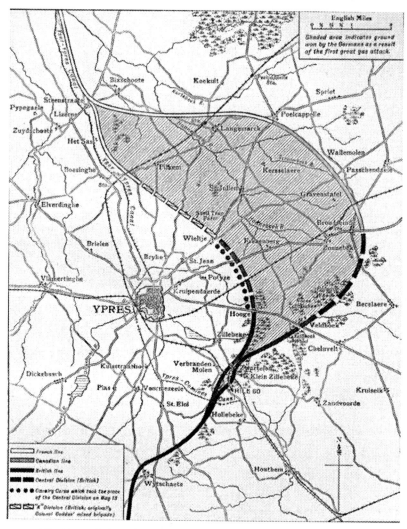

The Ypres Salient before and after the Second battle of Ypres,
April 22–May 13 1915

guess. Well now the days gradually dragged along, as they will do, and all preparations were made for the attack on that "clearing up" business which the Gen. spoke of. So I'll just tell you my part towards it and leave it to you. Mind you I'm not seeking bouquets, simply stating truths and someone said, "All men are liars". However, nearly all the night July 6th our guns of all sizes had been keeping it up, so I guess Fritz knew someone was going to get hurt before it was all over, and early in the morning on the 6th our lads went after him and some of his trenches. I forget how many prisoners came back but there were plenty killed and wounded and our lads got the trenches and held them against several counter-attacks. Of course we had also killed and wounded. At Brigade HQs we were kept busy dashing about with despatches and men and officers. Everyone was on duty that day of course. I know about 9 o clock that morning I heard the familiar cry "next out!" which meant next out for a message run. Well I was next out so the Sgt on duty said "an officer and twenty men with bombs has to be taken to the Battalion HQs in action, away you go."

They had a saying in France that it was better to be on your own than to have company [reference to lice], and I know very well I would sooner have been "on my own" than have the company of 20 men loaded with bombs. Fritz was now shelling all the tracks and hedges that led up to the scene of the attack as he was counter-attacking to regain his lost trenches and wanted to stop any reinforcements coming up from our side, so I had to lead these 20 men all through the shells dropping up to Battalion HQ's, with bombs in slings hanging around them, and in boxes. It was very hot weather and I only had a rifle and 50 rounds of ammunition, but I was sweating streams, so God knows how the other lads were feeling. Well by plenty of luck, plenty of dodging and ducking, walking and running from one tree to another, and constantly explaining to the officer where Fritz could see us and where he couldn't, I eventually got the whole lot across the open country to the more or less sheltered canal bank. But it was by no means the end of our journey, just about half way, but as we had a bit of cover we stayed for a breather. After about a 10 minute rest the officer asked if they were ready, and we moved along the canal bank with the shells now screaming over our heads on to the ground we had crossed. I told them we had near enough half a mile to go with little hell waiting for us when we got to the bridge, a wooden bridge thrown across the canal in full view of Fritz who could do what he liked.

We got to one end of the bridge and had to wait huddled up close to the bank as Fritz was getting really spiteful, and I certainly did not expect to get them across without someone getting hit. I said to the officer "When Fritz stops dropping them quite so thick, I'm going to dash across that bridge to see if the trench the other side is empty or full of troops". As I thought if I went with a rush of lads over the bridge to the trench just the other side and it was packed full with waiting reinforcements or troops waiting to come across the bridge the 20 I was responsible for would have to stand in the open, and me with them, and get blown to bits. So having fully explained to the officer, and heard him tell it to all the men, I had a smoke and wondered if it would be my last on earth. About 20 minutes had gone by now, so as Fritz was still sending 'em across at intervals, I asked the officer to time them. And we discovered there was just 40 seconds from one salvo to another. So just as soon as one lot had dropped I made a dash across like a hare and as I jumped down into the trench a Scotch voice said "Och man, Ha'e ye joost come across the bridge the noo?" And I said "Och eye". So we all laughed together. Then one of them said "It's a mercy ye're not kilt entirely, I would not go across yon bridge for all the Generals in the Army". But I expect he would if Fritz had shelled him. I said, "Is there plenty of room up the trench?" and got the reply "Yes". So having explained that I had 20 men and all loaded and all waiting to dash across the bridge the Jocks moved further up the trench, and I sent a signal across to them to rush over in pairs between the shell salvos. They came like a stampeding herd of elephants about a dozen of them and nearly wrecked the bridge, because it was rather shaky owing to the attention Fritz was paying it with gun fire. As soon as they were all across safe we went on up the canal on the other side until I got them to the Battalion HQs. They were told to put their bombs down and clear out, as there was no cover of any sort if Fritz started shelling again, and he had only just stopped as we arrived.

They needed no second telling so within 5 minutes they and me were all filing back the way we had come. We reached the bridge again to find Fritz still amusing himself, so we went across in the same manner we had previously used and so got to the far side without any casualties. Then along the canal again to the open country which we doubled across in quick time to the farm. When we were nearing the farm I was walking with the officer just at the head of his men, he turned to me and said "Thank you very much orderly for the way you handled us going up and coming back. I think it was jolly smart", "have a gasper" [I think he was a full blown second lieutenant just out from home]. Anyway he had not previously been in that part of the line, nor had his men as they were reserve from another part of the line, ready to be used as reinforcements if needed, and, of course, he did not know his way and my job as an orderly was to get him and his men up there and back which I did. And although it has not taken a long time to write it, it took nearly three hours to do it under constant shellfire. So I ask you, did those lads and myself earn a medal that day? Of course we did, but we did not get it for the simple reason that jobs like that and others as bad or worse, were being done every day, just the same as going to work every day, only where those who went to work in England each day during the war had a wage to come at the end of the month, we had a shilling a day for our job. Queer world this!

CHAPTER 10

First Spell on the Somme

So much for the Pilkhem attack of July 6th 1915. Well now when every thing was satisfactorily settled from the British point of view [I don't know whether Fritz was satisfied. I don't really think he could have been as he was always trying to get his trenches back by raiding them], we were taken out of the line after being relieved by a London Division just out from England, all brand new. Our Brigade went back some miles to two villages called Houtherge and Watou for a rest. I think we stayed there about a fortnight or three weeks, and then entrained for the Somme, eventually arriving at Doullens[22] early in August 1915. We had a short stay at Beauval, about 5 kilometres from Doullens, and moved off one morning by road and marched about 20 or 30 kilometers to a place called Englebelmet up near Albert[23]. There we found we were taking over a sector of the line from the French troops, and evidently down around that part they did not know there was a war on in 1915 [bet they did in '16!]. Things were so quiet when we arrived that the French troops used to sit knitting socks and scarves and hang their blankets on the barbed wire in "no man's land" to air 'em. We were amazed especially after the "hot shop" we had just left in Belgium. I know some very unkind things were said about the French government using up all the British troops to free France and putting her own troops in quiet parts of the line. The trenches there were 600 yards apart in some places. The orchards were full of fruit, estaminets open in the village, and plenty of civvies in the villages around, so that "being in the line" there was as good as being back "at rest". Well after we had relieved the French division holding that part of the line, and we got settled there, the Brigade HQs suddenly discovered that they were too far back from the Battalion HQs so one day we had to pack up and move to the village named Martinsart which was about a mile from Fritz's lines as the "crow flies", or to be more exact, "as the shell flies", so we were nicely in range of Fritz's guns once more [thanks very much], and of course when we got our guns in position, they found they had more ammunition than they needed, so without asking Fritz if he could do with it, they sent him some carriage paid. So what couldn't Fritz do but return the compliment and so you see upset all the "entente cordiale" which had taken root between Frenchie and Fritz. That's the worst thing about the British Artillery. They always want to be throwing their weight around. There was a little village called Mesnil up in the front of us on a bit of a hill with "civvies" living there nice and comfortable, while the French troops had been holding the line, but when our guns invited Fritz to "pull his socks up", Fritz soon sent a few rounds into Mesnil that had the effect of an order for all civilians to pack up their goods and move elsewhere. One young French woman had a nasty scar over her right eye from a piece of Jerry shellfire.

Well now we just at this time the Signal Section had to find extra signallers to occupy a post known in signalling language as "Report Centre". So I was told, along with a Corporal Watson and 3 others, to go to Report Centre as a "telephone linesman", work which consisted of repairing all telephone lines belonging to our Brigade which ran across country from Brigade HQ's to Report Centre to the 2 battalions in the line. We were posted about half a mile from Martinsart the village where Brigade HQ finally settled down, and about half of a mile from Battalion HQs. Just on the hill behind us was Mesnil Village, and we made our home in a bank about 300 yards from Mesnil at the junction of a forked road, We were not very comfortable there for the first couple of weeks, but after our artillery had shelled Fritz a bit, and Fritz had replied by shelling Mesnil, the order came for the civvies to clear out of Mesnil, and plenty of them left some very useful things behind. So we had a prowl round one day and "borrowed" a few things. A kitchen range, table, chairs, some windows and curtains complete, and a lot of pots and pans were loaded up on a cart, which we "found" in one of the yards, and taken to our dugout in the bank. So after we had been there about a month I tell you, I would not have changed places with the Brigadier at HQ. Also we went up to the Mesnil one night and raided a pigeon loft, which had about 50 pigeons in it. You can guess what happened to the pigeons [fairly tender some of them were]. Well now we were in this sector of the line from August 1915 to February 1916, so you may guess we had to get changed round a bit, to give each of our lads a fair share of the rough and smooth. So after about 2 months at Report Centre, I got put back at Brigade HQ again as cycle orderly, a job of cycling about the country with messages for different people. And it was on one of my rides back to Englebelmet that I witnessed as fine a bit of air fighting as anyone could wish for.

I was riding gaily along the dusty road when I suddenly heard a "pop-pop-pop" away up in the air. I looked up and saw one of the Fritz big bombers and one of our little fast ones getting at it. I reckon I watched that fight for half an hour, and I bet it was watched by thousands of eyes. Talk about "hawk" v "sparrows", they were no where near it for flying, swerving and gliding in the air, now dropping now climbing, manoeuvring all the while for position to open at one another with their machine guns. First our little one would fire a quick burst, rat a tat, then Fritz would fire a slower one, till suddenly our little one climbed quick and got just behind Fritz's plane, and sent such a stream of bullets right into him, and the big bomber slid away to earth in a long slant and dropped over a mile away from where he started. It was just like a shooting star gliding down at night. It dropped near a village called Headuville where a battalion of our Brigade were back at rest, so I hopped on my bike again and rode like the devil for the spot. When I arrived the plane was in a mess, and surrounded by our troops from the village. The pilot and observer were, of course, stone dead, covered with blood. I heard a wallet was found on one of them, a photo of a very nice looking girl in it, maybe his wife or sweetheart, I know I felt darned sorry for her, but I suppose that's all in the war. Evidently our chap got away with it alright, as I heard he landed a little distance off and came over to see his handiwork. When he saw it he saluted it and said "poor chaps".

Well now I had been about two hours too long on my journey so I hopped on the bike and pushed off back to Brigade with the news. Later it became an everyday occurrence to see planes fall, some crash, and some in flames. I had about a month at Brigade HQs as orderly, and was then sent to a place called Hamel. Another hot shop, as Fritz was on the hill overlooking the village, and he made it very uncomfortable getting about during daylight. He was very fond of sniping. Next to the village was a big ravine called the "Y" ravine because of its shape, and which figured largely in the Somme offensive later on. We were about 2 or 3 miles from Martinsart by the route we had to take, so we used to go in pairs to fetch our rations each night from Report Centre where they were brought for us. We had a big deep trench dug up one side of the hill for reliefs and reinforcements to come up and down, and as the infantry in the line used to change over every 4 nights on account of it being a "hot-shop", consequently the trench was nearly always occupied by passing troops of some mob or other. Working parties, reliefs, ration parties and all that had to use the same trench, and used to climb out of the trench and walk along the top if the moon was not too bright, but we always had to keep near the trench ready to dive from shell or machine gun fire. Still it wasn't so bad taking it all round. I remember one night though when one of our chaps turn came to go on leave, and Brigade forgot to send another in his place; that left 3 of us to work the post for a couple of days. Two men had to be constantly on duty, one to take messages from the Battalion over the phone, and the other to go out and repair the lines if shellfire broke them. So that left only one to go back for rations. The Corporal said he would go himself, so off he went. He got to the RC alright and got the rations, but in the meantime Fritz had made a big impression on the trench with a few heavy shells just after he passed, so on the way back he found a big hole had to be jumped to get pass, and as he thought he might spill the "rum ration" if he jumped and fell down, he calmly drunk all three rations of rum for safety, and told us what he'd done when he arrived. Course we did not say much to him, bet your life.

Talking of leave reminds me one day I was on my way back to Brigade HQs when I spotted a party of about 8 men going back to the rail-head to get the train for leave to England, but they never reached it as a German aeroplane dropped a bomb smack amongst them as they were marching and "got the lot". Hard lines that. It made me sweat.

Well now the usual change over came round in due course, and I once more found myself back at Report Centre again, this time as operator. Now listen here reader, a few pages back I told you how I did not get a medal, also I said I would tell you how some people got their medals. I'll do so now. As I have just mentioned, this time I was an operator at RC, and while on duty one day I received a call from Brigade to put him through to a certain battalion, which shall remain nameless [but they wear black buttons on their tunics]. 'Twas the Brigade Major speaking and I'm not betraying any operator by saying that all operators kept themselves "plugged in" to overhear any conversations [which is a well known secret]. I'll tell you that when I had got the Adjutant of the black-buttoned regiment on the phone and the "B.M" on the other end, I kept my plug in and this is what I heard. "Is that you Bubbly?" "I say, I have got to send in a few names of any officers of the Brigade or NCOs and men, who have done anything noticeable during the last few weeks. Mind you there are only a very few medals to be served out, so if you have any special pal that you want to have a medal, don't put his name at the bottom of the list, or he will be unlucky. D'you get me". The Adjutant answered, "OK quite". Then he went on to say "That being the case I am certainly going to put my batman at the top of the list, as he is a perfect gem at cooking eggs and bacon and scrounging hot shaving water, etc etc.". So I hope the batman is wearing the DCM or the VC for something different than cooking hen fruit and rashers of pig. When I heard those two officers talking like that, I was tempted to pull the plugs out and stop their gassing. But it gives the reader of this narrative some idea of how some people got their medals. I'm well aware that many hundreds who are wearing 'em, won 'em, also some who are wearing 'em don't know what they got them for, such as the baker at the Base who had a DCM for baking bread. Distinguished conduct!

Leave Christmas 1915

Well, now I've told you something let's get on again. We are now getting very near Christmas 1915, so one day I took a message while on duty concerning no one else but "your truly", to the effect that I should be going home on leave about Christmas Day. And on Christmas Eve I had another message telling me to be at Brigade HQs at 5 pm next day for a lift back to the railhead at Acheux. I slept well on the message you bet, and was up early next morning. As I was considered off duty all Christmas Day, I volunteered to go down to Martinsart and get the things for Christmas dinner. We had a very good cook attached to us, and I have had worse Christmas dinners back in England before now than the one that we had that day. Well on my way back to the village I stopped and had chat with some gunners of a heavy battery who were sitting about by their guns, and about 100 shells were stacked near at hand. I asked if they were a present for Fritz for Xmas, and a Bombardier said they had orders not to fire any at all that day unless Fritz started the ball rolling, then they were going to fire "that lot" pointing to the stack of big shells. I told them I was going on leave that afternoon, and they called me a "lucky gent" and a few more things too unladylike to mention, and I went down to the village and got the Christmas "pudding" [some of "Ticklers" or "Woolworths", I'm not sure which]. We made a champion dinner and washed it down with English beer, rum, and champagne, and felt all merry and bright, thank you, and about 4pm, I packed up and started off for Brigade again, very well pleased with myself. Well now, I was humming a tune as I was mooching along the trail to the village feeling pleased with world, for Fritz and everyone, when without any warning four shells screamed over my head and landed smack into Martinsart where I had to go. I thought, "I'm dammed who told Fritz I was going on leave". I was about a mile from the village so I thought I would stay where I was for a few minutes and let him have his spite out and then go on. Fritz sent over a few more and then our artillery opened out and I had a nice little half hours picnic watching a bombardment. Fritz fired about 100 Xmas greetings, I guess. Well things quietened down at last and I got a move on to get my leave papers and money. I found that one "Jock" had been wounded and a mule killed. Good Luck. I made my way to where I knew Brigade HQs were billeted and found everyone merry and bright, all more or less "gassed" [drunk], and everyone in for "community singing". Plenty of beer, both English and French was flowing, champagne, red wine, white wine and rum, plenty of fags, and the remains of a big Christmas dinner on the table and on the floor. They had fixed up a table in a barn, and looted some furniture from the houses, and it looked like a respectable family gathering all ready to "bust". Of course I was promptly invited to "muck in" [help myself] which I did, and then I hunted around for the sergeant with the money and papers. I found him more or less "gassed" same as the rest, and then I had to "wait for the wagon" [that came about 9pm by the way; all drunk, even the donkey shaky]. So to use up the time I went fast back to where the wine was flowing, and made myself useful helping it to flow faster. I evidently dived deeper than I had intended, or got out of my depth somehow, as I can only remember getting thrown into the wagon when it was empty and that woke me up.

I had chummed up with some more men who were coming home, so about 9pm Christmas Night 1915 we started off for England from the Somme. I must have dozed off in the wagon as I next found myself in a railway yard lying on the cobblestones shivering with cold about 5am Boxing morn. Talk about cold, the North Pole was a heat wave compared to it; at least that's how I felt. We had to wait for the leave train now, and I

The Golden Madonna on the Basilica. It was hit by German shellfire in
January 1915 but did not fall. One legend was that the War would end on the
day it fell to the ground.

for one had a mind to pack off back to where I had come from. I never felt
so cold and fed up in my life as I did on that cold Boxing morning in the
goods yard at Acheux. I would have cheerfully given all my furlough
money for a first cup of coffee. Anyway all good and bad things come to
an end, and the leave train eventually came backing in, and troops from all
different parts climbed aboard. We sat shivering in the trucks for about half
an hour, and when the driver finally decided that we were all frozen to
death he obligingly started. Now I have had a few hundred train rides in
several different parts of the world, but I think French trains and their
whole railway system is the limit. Speaking from experience I reckon the
Chinese could give France points on the railway wagons and lines.
However after spending a whole day and a night cooped up in a cattle van

like sardines, we crawled down to Havre about dawn and had to go to camp till night time came, as it appears leave boats only crossed in the dark. Perhaps they were ashamed of their "cargo". Anyway we were glad to have an opportunity to shave and wash, as I had not have a wash since I left the dugout on Christmas Day, and now it was the 27th. So we had a "dig out" and hung around in this camp, forbidden to go here or there, forbidden to do this or that, till most of us felt like saying, "Damn the leave". There was a lot more freedom "in action" up the line than there was at Base. Too much "red tape" and too many Red Caps were in use down there. Well we did eventually get aboard a boat and slipped across to Southampton fairly early on the 28th December, and we soon got away on a good old "Blighty" train for our respective towns and villages.

I had eight days leave and re-joined the Brigade HQ at Martinsart about the 10th January 1916, and was kept there as orderly for a week or two.

CHAPTER 11

The Somme 1916

Well, as you all know the big offensive on the Somme took place from July 1st 1916, but preparations began months before as you may guess, so a part of the general scheme was for our division to attack at or near the place where we had been in the line for nearly 7 months. So early in February the whole division was taken out of the line and our Brigade went right away back to Beauval again, somewhere between 30 or 40 kilometres in the rear. We had roughly a month there squaring up and getting reinforced and when all was ready we relieved some division in the line at Fonguevilliers[24] and Hennescamp just north of the old sector. On the way up by road the transport was heavily shelled and one unlucky wagon had a direct hit right between two horses, as they were moving along the road with the column. They were just ahead of the party I was with and when we came up there was a sickening sight. One horse had it's head and neck taken clean off, and the other poor devil was blown completely in halves with two legs and half a body 4 or 5 yards from the front legs and head. The driver was killed and the chap sitting up beside them had a leg off. That happened near St Armand.

The Brigade selected Bienvilliers as the best village for their purpose and we had quite a long stay there. The front line trenches ran through the villages of Fonquevilliers and Hennescamp, about $3/4$ mile straight across open country, and Fritz could see everything from his "sausage balloons". One day he let us know he could see all by bursting a shell over a field just near the village while we were playing a football match between Brigade HQ and the Transport. Luckily no one was hit but the match did not finish that day. Perhaps Fritz was jealous of us having a game of football, or he wanted to score a goal with a shell. We were mostly employed in this part of the line in digging cable trenches 6ft deep from Bienvilliers to the

The Allied lines from the Sea to Rheims in June 1916

two Battalions' HQs in preparation for the Somme battle. There must have been hundreds of miles of cable buried on the Somme if all the divisions buried as much as ours did. We were at it for weeks in different places. After a while we were taken back some distance again for "recuperation", I just forgot the name of the place now, but nothing very important happened during our stay with the exception of a lot of unnecessary parades and inspections, till the date arrived when we had orders to move into line for the Somme "big push".

We arrived one day by road at a village called Mailley-Maillet just north again of our old place, and found the country around simply teeming with troops, among them being the 29th Division from the Dardanelles. We knew that there was some dirty work coming off at the crossroads. We were put into a forsaken chateau, which had received some help from Fritz towards falling to pieces. In peacetime it was no doubt a very fine house with large gardens well stocked at the back of it, [I'm sure the rent must have been more than 10/- per week and rates], and was evidently owned by someone with "tons of money", but who had now left for the benefit of their health on receipt of a "visiting card" from Fritz and his guns. It was well within range of Fritz's big guns, as we found out the same night when some of the lads went up to the bedrooms and lit a light to make a bed on the bedroom floor. Fritz objected, and the result was two very severely wounded Tommies on the first night. One was a motor despatch rider, the other a signaller. I heard later that the dispatch rider lost his leg.

We settled down in this chateau for our HQs and after the operators had been picked out the rest of us had the job of more cable trench digging; all night work, rain, rain, rain all day and all night. Some people used to say it was on account of the heavy gunfire, for it was continuous day and night for weeks. There was every type of gun being used then and 18 pounders were as common as daisies in a grass field. Anyway it simply rained torrents for days, and if anyone who has ever tried digging 6 ft deep trench on a dark night in blinding rain reads this, he knows then what I'm talking about. Still it had to be done at night or not at all, as Fritz would have wiped us of the map in daytime. As it was he used to shell in the night if he thought we were at it, and many a time we've had to dive down in the mud at the bottom of the trench for cover. So you may well guess we looked pretty every morning at dawn when we reached our billet. This went on for a couple of weeks and then we were taken a little way back in reserve to pull ourselves back together again.

And then one night at the end of June 1916 we moved up to a place near Sierre[25] crossroads just left of Beaumont–Hamel, the famous Y ravine[26] which I mentioned earlier and Thiepval[27] and the sights we saw on the way are beyond description. Guns, guns, guns. Wheel to wheel 18 pounders, 6 inch, 4.7's, Naval guns, Howitzers, 12 inch railways, and the Lord knows what else.

Thiepval Memorial to the missing of the Somme

Beaumont-Hamel from Hawthorne Ridge

I thought we had enough guns to blow Fritz to hell and back, but, and it's a big BUT, we didn't as you know.

Well now without putting in any frill or trimmings, I'll try to tell you what I know about the battle of the Somme. I was told to go from Brigade HQs with a chum of the RE signals to a battalion HQs and take all the messages for the battalion from Brigade and vice-versa. Sometime during the night of the 30th June, my pal and I could have been seen struggling up the trench called the Roman Road, on account of it's straightness. It was packed with troops of all descriptions knee deep in mud and slush in places, so you can guess it was no Sunday morning stroll. We did arrive at last after a devil of a struggle with the troops we passed in the trench. We reported ourselves to the Adjutant in a bit of a dugout about 10 ft square, and in it was the Colonel, Adjutant, a Major, a Sergeant, several orderlies, and my pal and I. So we had tons of room, I don't think. Then to make things more cheerful Fritz started dumping some trench mortars around the country and we had some in the trench just by the steps of our dugout which killed several of the regiment, and made several of those who were

From 8th Corps
To Brig. Gen. Prowse

Please convey to every officer, NCO, and men of the Old Stonewall Infantry Brigade the pleasure that their old commander and Brigadier, now their comrade and Corps Commander, feels at having them with him in the big fight. The old STONEWALLERS have always known how to stand heavy losses and to stick it out and to win through it to victory by hard fighting in the coming battle. The STONEWALLERS have the position of honour and will, I know, prove again as always that they are SECOND to NONE.

My heartfelt greetings and best wishes.

Aylmer Hunter-Weston

The last orders to the Stonewall Brigade before the 1st July

wounded seek cover in the steps and dugout of the Colonels. Oh! It was a lovely night, believe me. We found the wire, which ran to Brigade HQs and were overjoyed to find that it had not been "busted" by shellfire. Only

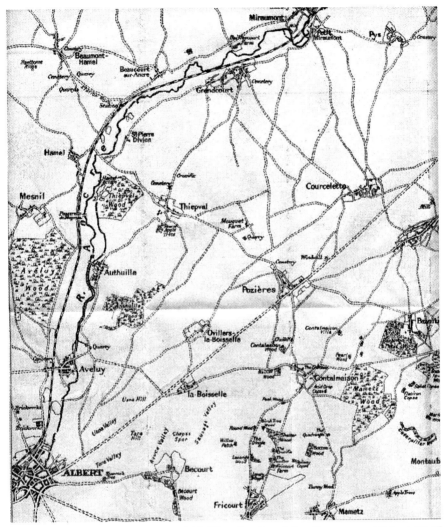

Map of the Somme from Philip Gibb's The Battle of the Somme *published 1917*

any lineman who has been put at night looking for a broken cable in a dose of shelling knows what it is to find he's through alright. Well our luck being in in that respect we proceeded to sort ourselves out the best way we could under the circumstances. Both huddled up in a corner trying to receive messages and praying the line would not get "busted", as Fritz was now shelling like mad, as though he had been told the trenches were packed with troops. There must have been an awful slaughter going on just around us and the "big stuff" fairly shook the dugout, and anyone direct hit would have buried us alive.

We all sat huddled together in this dugout, my pal and I taking and sending messages, and the officers talking together about their plans for the morning battle. As the time drew near for the "zero hour" which was to be at 7.30am [zero hour meant the time the boys went over the top], the officers had some spirits and a jar of rum was opened and served amongst the troops. [I've got something to say about rum later on which may surprise the readers of this diary]. Just now I'm writing of what I actually saw, later I'll tell you what others saw and told me. We few in the HQ dugout had a jar of rum between us, and had my chum and I drunk all that was offered us, we should have died of rum poisoning. As it was we had a pint enamel cup between two. Rum was never a favourite drink of mine, so I just sipped it to keep the cold out, and my pal had some for the same reason. Had we drunk it all I'm afraid very few messages would have been sent and accepted by us and that may have meant disastrous results for the troops "going over" and ourselves. I well remember the Adjutant picking up a glass of spirit and saying "Here's to the Hun when we meet him in the morning". Well the night wore on at last and near about the time for "going over" the Colonel and Major left the dugout. I've never seen them since, and they were both killed I heard later.

Well now what actually happened outside I do not know, but soon after "zero hour" one line back to the Brigade got "bust", and as my pal was taking a message it was up to me to take the spare phone and go back along the line and repair it, [when I found it]. Now I'm not going to forget the sights in a hurry that I saw coming along that hellhole of a trench. As soon as I got out into the trench from the dugout I was nearly killed by a shell dropping into the traverse behind me and lifting about 20 yards of the parapet and trench away. Machine gun fire, whizz-bangs, and heavy shells were flying about in all directions. Wounded men were lying in the bottom of the trench and some hanging over the side where they had been killed climbing out. Reinforcements coming up, stretcher-bearers, water parties, ammunition carriers, and a host of other parties, all mixed together in the trench. Wounded were moaning and getting hit again as they lay in the trench. I thought, "Gee, however am I going to find my cable amongst that lot?" It was absolutely impossible to walk in the trench without walking on dead or wounded so I clambered up the

Old trench lines and memorial to those Canadians who fell on July 1st 1916. Newfoundland Park, Beaumont–Hamel.

Casualty clearing station under fire near Trones Wood July 1916

side of the slimy muddy bank and pulled my cable up and ran it through
my hand as I slivered and stumbled along the top of the trench. I felt scared
to death, "honest Injun", but I had to repair that line, and I was praying all
the time that someone had been sent out from the other end to help. I felt
as sick as a dog with the smell of human blood all round and with hearing
the moan and groans of dying lads. Sometimes I fell down in shell holes,
half full of muddy water, and a dozen times or more I had to jump into the
trench to "unpeg" the cable, or dodge a shell. It was nearly $^3/_4$ of a mile
from Brigade to dugout [$^3/_4$ of a mile of hell with the lid off]. I had my
water bottle with me, and it was full when I started [a quart], but it was
empty before I got back and I did not sip it myself. If I could have carried
a ten-gallon tank on my back it would not have been sufficient to give
away to the lads who were wounded and asking for water. I gave all I had
to one or another, and I guess it was the last drink that many of them had
in this world.

At last I came to the end of my cable. So pegging it to the ground I had to grope around for the other end. A shell had made a hole large enough to put a town hall in [almost] so it was useless hoping to find the other end just there. I nipped around the crater and got to the trench again and tapped in on the first cable I found. No luck. Tried another, and found I was through to Brigade. That cheered me more than a £5 note would have done just then, and I now joined the piece of spare cable that I had brought with me and dashed around the shell hole to join up with the other end, and then I found I was "through" both ways. What a relief that was, as I fully expected it to be broken behind me where I had pulled it out of the trench all the way along, as it was now exposed to all shell fire that was freely dropping around. I thought to myself "Georgie boy, you've earned a smoke", so I get out my "gaspers" and lit up as best I could with my hands, face and khaki caked with yellow mud. As I knelt in this big shell hole puffing at my fag I had a good view of the attack just in front. And here's the picture as I saw it. The ground rose in front of me and I could see our troops dashing from one trench to another, some would drop down "forever" on the way, and some would be a trifle luckier. I saw heaps and heaps of dead bodies lying around in the open. On the right were several long lines of troops advancing across the open. At a steady trot, with several getting knocked out. Then I saw someone sending a message up in front, and I read "For God's sake send bombs" which was repeated again and again. Evidently some of our lads were in a tight corner, as we all were just then. Of course I knew I must not hang about there too long, as the cable may get broken elsewhere, also Fritz was making the countryside very unhealthy with his guns. So I started off back to the dugout, but as I got nearer he started a barrage all along the sector just between me and the dugout, which was too hot for a mouse to go through while it lasted, but without getting hit. I was thankful that it did not last long, about 20 minutes, but while it did I scrambled down into the trench amongst the wounded and dead, and had a chat with some of the wounded, and I'm going to tell you what I heard from some of those lads who "went over the top" at 7.30, and were now back in the trench wounded.

There were some of different regiments and as we sat there waiting for the barrage to lift I was told, amongst other things, that hundreds of our lads met their deaths "blind drunk with rum". I was told that heaps of them climbed out of the trench when "zero hour" came without rifle or equipment, some even without their "hats" on, and linking arms went out into "no man's land" singing "Tipperary" and "Pack up your troubles". Who says there was not too much rum now? Every man is entitled to his opinion, and my opinion is that we lost hundreds of the lives of our troops by "broadcasting" the "rum jar". Well now, I made my way back to my pal in the dugout and found him still "through", saints be praised, and we made a breakfast of fat cold pig, biscuits and water. I told him a few of things I had seen and heard during the last couple of hours and he said "What bist grousing about, we had a pint between us!" We stayed there all day and were relieved at night by two regimental signallers and had orders to make our way back to the Brigade. The trench was just as bad to come through then as it was in the morning, so as there was very little shelling going on but plenty of machine gun and rifle fire as we clambered out on the top. My pal had a smack by a bullet as soon as we got up, only it went sideways clean through his canteen slung over his back. Had it gone in direct from behind him it would have been through his lungs or somewhere.

We came to the shell hole where I had repaired the cable in the morning and stood peering down into it for a moment. I've thought of the "Better Ole" cartoons many times since that one.

We reached Brigade more or less alive, but dead beat, as we had been awake all the day before, all the night and all this day on a meal of fat meat, biscuits and water. So you bet we ate some and slept some the first chance we had. We held the line for a couple of days, and then got relieved and put out behind somewhere handy for a while. Coming back up the trench called the Roman Road was like walking along a riverbed, mud, slime and slush all the way. We were moved up again in a few days and it was while in the line this time that I heard of a sad occurrence. It appears that some of our chaps were roaming about in no man's land out of their minds over what they had been through for the last week or more, and the Padre had gone out with a small patrol to try and get some of them in to our trenches. Everyone, with "one exception" had been warned about the patrol going out, and it appears the patrol were successful in finding a couple of crazed lads[28] and were making their way to our lines at night with them. But "the exception" was a machine gun post which had not been warned and, of course, seeing a party of men coming from the direction of the enemy trenches promptly opened fire and killed them all. I should think it's very true, as no one in their senses would invent a yarn like that. And it could so easily have happened after the line was broken on the Somme.

[On 1 July 1916, the first day of the battle of the Somme, VIII Corps suffered the highest casualties of any corps and achieved nothing. It spent much of the remainder of the war in quiet sectors and back areas. During that time Private Coward was with the Royal Engineers, to whom he was permanently transferred in May 1917, as the brief section from his war record shows.]

Brief "respite" in Belgium

Well we held the line there for about a week and then were taken right away back and after a rest and reinforcements had been sent to different regiments, we entrained about this time and finally found ourselves up at Dunkirk splashing about on the Belgium coast. The yarn was flying around that we were going to make an attack on Zeebrugge. We could see our Monitors out at sea shelling Zeebrugge and once we saw some Zepps returning from a raid.

Back to the Somme

Why we went there I never found out, but after about a month doing nothing, we entrained again and went back to the Somme. This time we went in action up near Delville Wood and Trones Wood, and had Brigade HQs at a place called Bricqueterie. 'Twas there that I saw the Prince of Wales one misty morning strolling about just as Fritz had dumped over a few long range shells from the direction of Bapaume.

Our Brigade's infantry were in action at the cemetery at Sailly-Sailleul, which Fritz had made into a little fort among the tombstones. We are now somewhere about November 1916, so after a smack at Fritz up there for a

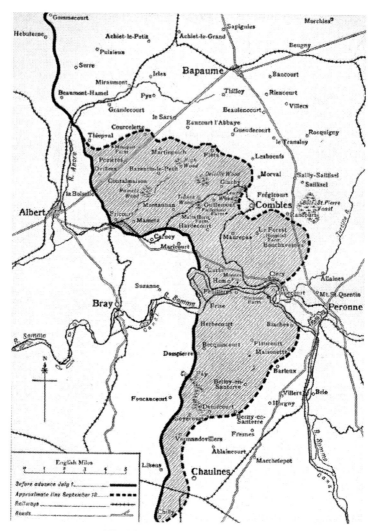

Allied Battlefield on the Somme,
showing gains from July 1st to September 28th 1916

week or two we were pushed back out of it again.

While we were in action up there I'd like to mention how a poor kid named Meadows died. His father was the Postmaster at Epsom, I believe at the time. He was a big strapping lad about 19 or 20 years old I guess, and as good-natured a lad as you would meet. He always shared his parcels from

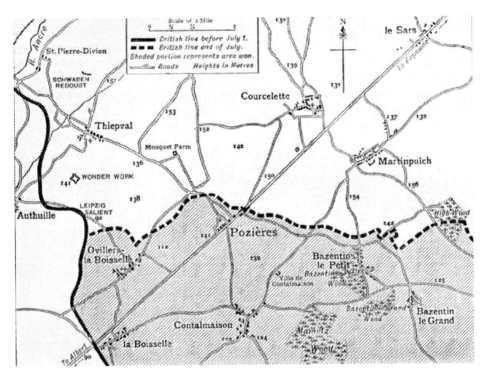

The Battle of the Somme; position of the British line at the end of July 1916

home with his pals. Well now, we were in a place just then where dugouts were scarce as they were in the beginning of the war, so we had to make the best of it. Young Meadows and a pal of his named Boston, both RE signallers, got a sheet of corrugated iron from somewhere and laid it across boxes to make a better shelter for the night out in the open somewhere as they had been out "scrounging" and all the "safest" places were taken. During the night Fritz started shelling us heavily, but no one apparently knew that these two had slept under that sheet of tin. In the morning they were missing from breakfast, and a hunt was made for them, and we found them under the tin more dead than alive. It was raining, pouring, as the chum and I dashed for a stretcher, and four of us put poor Meadows on and laid him on his stomach as I honestly believe that had we laid him on his back his whole inside would have rolled out. His arm was laid open from just below his elbow to his wrist, and his left hand was hanging off. Poor kid. He was unconscious of course. Four other pals carried Boston away [he recovered], and three pals and myself carried poor young

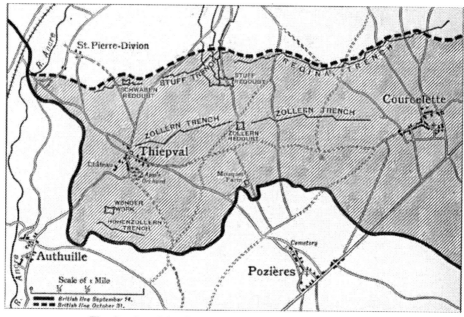

*The Battle of the Somme; positions on Thiepval Ridge,
September 14th–October 31st 1916*

Meadows. It was raining hard, blowing a gale [which saved us from getting gassed, by the way], and once we had "waders" on and our goggles, so you can guess the "going" was treacherous. Fritz started shelling with gas shells and that made us put on our goggles, the rain made us put on our waders and consequently we were slipping about all over the place with this poor kid on the stretcher. We should surely have been gassed if the high wind had not blown the stuff away as soon as the shells burst, and they were dropping all around us as true as I write this. The jolting young Meadows was getting must have aroused him as he said in a feeble voice "Put something under my head". By a bit of luck we were just passing some ruined dugouts, so spotting an old blanket that had been used to keep the gas out, we laid him gently down and I slivered across the mud and got it. We carefully raised his head and laid it on the dirty, rotten, soaking, wet blanket. But it was the very best we could do, as there were no other troops near us, and time was too precious to keep him waiting about owing to the state he was in, and we had no idea how far we may have to go to find any first aid post. As a matter of fact we did not find one, but hailed an ambulance motor, which was coming up a track between the shell holes. He saw the state the poor kid was in and turned back at once. While he was skidding about trying to turn the car round among the shell holes which took a bit of doing, we laid poor Meadows on the ground to rest him and he just whispered "Turn me on my back, I can't get my breath". But we dare not turn him over on account of his wounds. We put him in the ambulance and I heard he died soon after. The other one got over his, and as far as I know, he is alive now. Now we got off back to the dugout, and cussed Fritz all the way back, as we were fond of Meadows.

Well now, in due course we were taken out of the line again, and went back somewhere near Bray, and it is getting much nearer to Christmas 1916.

Nothing much happened while we were back at rest, with exception of long-range shelling by Fritz, or a few bombs from his planes at times, but that was mere detail to what we got up in front.

Anyway while at Bray[29] I was informed my turn would be due for leave while out at rest. And on the 4th January 1917 I arrived in England after going through the usual procedure of French troop trains once more. On my return to France in January I was sent to an outstation with a pal of mine near Peronne and Bouchavenes, A nice healthy spot up the "Death Valley". The name gives the game away. We took over from some French troops again and were in a hole on the side of a bank about 20ft high. On the top of the bank right over our heads were a pair of French 75s, and one day Fritz hit one clean over the edge of the bank. We were now having terribly cold weather, and I well remember the agony of getting a shave and wash. We two were there for a fortnight and then relieved by two more and went into Brigade HQ yet again. The Brigade moved HQs after a while and this same pal [Fowler his name, killed at Fampoux near Arras 1918], and the Brigade pigeon flyer, found a bit of a sunken road, which we "took over for home". It was an entrance to a German dugout that had been dug in the earth for about 10ft then abandoned. Some straw and old blankets were in it so we thought they'd do to make a bed. Sorry we thought so after, as we got as "lousy as a rat". Soon after we three occupied the place and had made ourselves as comfortable as the lice etc, would permit, I had a big parcel come from home, Xmas pudding, and mince pies, a cake and several odds and ends, and we had a nice little blow-out one night, just the three of us crouching round a charcoal brazier which we pinched. Almost as soon as we had finished the Corporal of the Signals on duty pulled the blanket aside that hung over the entrance to keep gas out [but it wouldn't have] and said "Whose next out?" that meant that a line had been broken somewhere and it had to be repaired at once. I said I was next out "Damn you". He said we looked as if we had been enjoying ourselves, which we had. So I said, "What line is busted", and was told the "left battalion". Fowler said he would come out with me in return for the "blow–out" he had just shared, so getting on gas masks, field telephone, spare cable, and tape, flash lamp etc etc, Fowler and I hit the trail.

I took the end of the cable in my hand from the signal dugout and found it ran all across country somewhere in the direction of the shelling which had gone on earlier in the night. It was pitch dark and coming from the lighted dugout we could not see our own noses when we looked down on 'em. We heard two or three shells whining over, and an occasional burst of machine gun fire, otherwise all was quiet and still for a wonder. As I said I had the cable in my hand letting it slide through as I stumbled along and poor old Fowler was slushing along behind me also holding the cable, but although we could hear each other gliding along in the mud about 3 yards apart we could not see one another. We were in a new part of the line that neither of us had been over before and, of course, we had no idea of which direction to take other than the cable in our hands, and after going some considerable distance my cable suddenly ended and dropped in the mud. I promptly yelled "Whoa" to make him stop walking so that he should not lose his end. We both knew our jobs of course. His now was to hang on to that end and not lose it, mine was to crawl through the mud and find the other end, make a nice join and go back home to bed. Sounds all right don't it? But those that have done it know the difference between practicing and preaching. For a start as soon as I moved off I slid down the shell hole made by the shell that burst the cable, and I could smell the reeking fumes of the shell now. Of course that was a dry hole so I went across and up the other side thinking I might be lucky enough to find the other end of cable in the dark, but my luck was out. Every now and again my pal would call out "All right kiddie?" as we had arranged to do, and I would answer "Yes, so far", or something else as the case may be.

Fritz had been dumping them over pretty thick earlier in the night as the ground was simply a lot of holes interlaced one with another. The older shell holes were full of water, and I did not mind falling into the new ones as they were dry, although they stank of shell fumes, but I went twice into holes both 3 parts full of water, up to my waist once, and I once bumped into a dead body in one of them. Whether it was British, German or French I did not know and did not stay long enough to look closer. Yet another "cheerful friend" was a whole leg that had been blown off a Fritz, as I could tell by the jackboot. I seemed to be finding everything else but the end of this dammed cable, which I had to find. Then it suddenly occurred to me that I had not heard the arranged signal from my pal lately, so I gave a little shout and got no answer, gave another with the same results. Now reader what would you have done if you had been in my place? Imagine a pitch black night in a strange place, shell holes and all around you, some old, some new, the knowledge that Fritz might start shelling again any minute and blow you to bits, you've got to find a lost cable, and you've got to find your chum who might be wounded somewhere or perhaps dead, as plenty of stray bullets had been moaning over while we were out.

I called again, and getting no answer I started back in what I thought was the way I had come, and every now and then I would give a "stage shout", and after what appeared to be a month I saw what I thought was his flash light faintly glowing lying on the ground to my left. I called again and getting no answer I made a dive through a shell hole of water tearing my hand and coat on a stake with barbed wire on it, and dropped down to touch the flash lamp as I thought. Now reader do not shudder if you happen to be a lady, but that "flash lamp" was the face of a dead Fritz that was shining phosphorous in the night light, and I "smeared" my hand across it before I discovered my mistake. There were several lying around and had evidently been there since the battle as they were getting all bloated up. By now I was getting desperate as I could not find the cable or my chum, so I chanced my arm and let out a good yell, and heard a faint "Hello" in some direction, and started making for it, giving a "yelp" every now and then to make sure I was going right. We eventually met only to discover that we were as far off as ever, as he had lost his end of the cable through thinking the same about me, viz, that I had been shot and came back to look for me when he could not make me hear by "shouting quietly". We laughed together and then swore at each other in turns when neither of us knew which direction to get back to Brigade HQs to start again. I told him about the dead Fritzs lying about, and he only said, "Why didn't you bring back a helmet?" I had a mind to hit him on top of his head just for luck. We had a walk round in the dark trying to find our bearings and suddenly spotted some troops going to the left battalion with rations and enquired from them the way back to Brigade HQs. They did not know, much obliged. Thank you for nothing. To make a long story short we did manage to find a track which led somewhere and following it we found ourselves in the sunken road where Brigade HQ were in about a quarter of a mile away. All this wandering about had taken up some time, so on arrival at the signallers dugout we found that the battalion signallers had come out from their end to look for the break and had had almost the same trouble themselves when they came to the shell holes as the cable had been broken in a dozen places or more and was blown all over the place. They had given it up as bad job and had, by luck, found their way back to Brigade HQs to wait for our return. The Sergeant decided as it was dawn in a couple of hours to run out a new line in that part as soon as it was light enough to see. So we were laying a new cable almost before daybreak that morn.

Bray-sur-Somme

We are now in January or February 1917 and we had about three weeks in the sunken road dugout and were then relieved and came back around Bray- sur-Somme once more. It was bitter cold weather I know, and in the town of Bray there was a fine old house with big grounds and artificial lakes in the grounds which were all frozen over around the sides, but the centre was free of ice, and there were dozens of moorhens and other water fowl. We decided to have some for dinner one day, so half a dozen of us surrounded one of the smaller lakes armed with stones and short sticks. One threw a stone amongst the birds to get them to rise and whichever way they flew I or the other lad could fetch down one or two by throwing amongst them as they flew up. We kept this up for several days and always used to "win" anything from 10 to 20 waterfowls according to our luck, till one day those blinking "nosey parkers", the "Red Caps", came down and nabbed us. They took all our names, numbers and regiments, but that did not worry us much as we moved from Bray in a couple of days after. Now just to show you what a good poulterer I am I'll tell you that when I got back to the billet one day with 4 or 5 moorhens for dinner, we told "Bobagee", our cook, that he could have a couple of them if he would

An out of action English tank near Thiepval, September 1916

cook the rest for us. He was willing provided I plucked them, "as he was too busy to pick —— moorhens". So I set about pulling the feathers out and after nearly wearing out my finger tips trying to get some very fine, furry feathers off that seemed to be growing at the roots of the large ones, I chucked the dammed moorhen on the ground and told the cook he could have the lot as I couldn't pick these "blasted" small feathers off for nuts. He said "No, and if thee' bide there trying till the end of the war thee oosent do it, as thee's got to skin the last bit off". There was a covering of down which I was trying to pick off and couldn't so he got a knife and skinned it off, and all was well again.

But it reminds me of the time I went to the garden in the Aisne Valley in Sept 1914, to get some artichokes for dinner once. I was leaning against the high stems and asked another chap, who was looting some carrots, where these blinking artichokes were that everyone was looting and cooking. He said something about if "they blinking give way", "what thee bist leaning against, thee bist fall down on 'em"; how was I to know they had long stems? I thought I was in a bed of sunflowers, and that artichokes were things one bought at greengrocer's shops. However, everyone learns, and I still believe in the French motto "Honi soi qui mal 'y pense".

CHAPTER 12

Arras: Spring 1917

So let's get back again. After another spell at Bray we were moved back for the battle of Arras[30] that commenced Easter Monday 1917. We finally landed at a village called Dieval near St Pol, in the Pas de Calais and after a reformation of some troops and several of the usual inspections,[31] we moved up one day in a blinding snowstorm for the Arras attack. Will I ever forget that treck up to the attack in blinding snow, hail and rain at Easter 1917? Bet your life I won't in a hurry. We "went over" just left of Arras near the Scarpe river. And a fine old mess it was when the snow melted and turned the country into a sea of mud. That's where I heard many South African troops died of cold alone, and I don't wonder at it, as it was cold enough to kill a battalion of "esquimeauxs". We had the same old job of keeping communication between the regiments and Brigade, and some job it was too. We set up a "visual signal post" at one place on account of the Brigade having to keep on the move, and the uselessness of laying cable, but Fritz soon bumped us out of that with some big shells. Then we found a concrete dugout of Fritzs where he had been driven out, and the big shells of our guns had blown the trench in all around it, and we had to crawl in the opening on our hands and knees. We used that for a couple of days, and then had to clear out as it was gradually sinking into the mud. On the way up, I well remember turning the corner of a trench and seeing a Fritz sitting bolt upright at the top of the steps leading down to his dugout, and with his head spit open from his eyes to the back of his head, just as if someone had done it with a big axe; just a common sight out here. But I did not stand there sympathising with him as Fritz's guns were busy all the time, and don't forget that when possible we had to dive for cover or drop flat dozens of times. We came to the railway embankment running, I think, from Arras to Lens, and a tunnel running under it was well packed with wounded British and Germans.

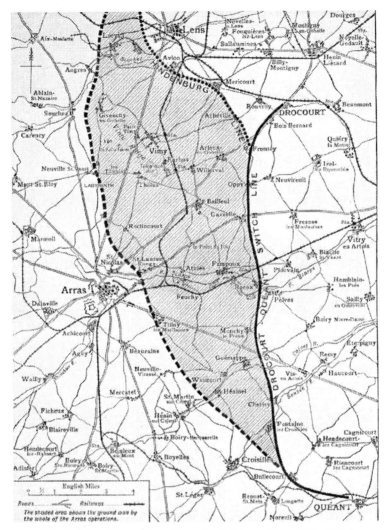

The Battle of Arras; lines from April 9th to May 17th 1917

The weather about this time began to brighten, consequently Fritz was busy with his aircraft, and some thrilling air fights took place just over our heads with various kinds of luck, in which, from my point of view "Jack was as good as his master", regardless of the fact that it used to appear in the papers that that several thousand [more or less] German planes were brought down on such and such a date, while the British and French lost about 10, say. That was for your benefit in England. Had you asked "us" we could have told you a different tale. The British had some good airmen, admitted, but then so did old Fritz.

Well let's get on with the story. The battle of Arras did not, as you know, take us to Berlin, altho' maybe it helped, as did the Somme, and all the rest of the battles, and we were held up, as you doubtless know. So after a spell in action maybe for a week or so, we were taken out of the line and brought back near Arras in reserve. After a rest we went up again, this time on the other side of the River Scarpe between the main Arras-Cambrai road and the Scarpe. Just in front of us on a hill top was Monchy-le-Preux, a little hell of a place for the infantry up there. And when Fritz had been driven out of it he just about gave it something to remember him by. He used to dump all his spare big shells on poor old Monchy. We were in some of his old dugouts just on the level ground between Monchy and Arras, and had a nice view of the Vimy Ridge across the Scarpe River. The usual routine was operating lineman or otherwise, in turn for about a month. The transport lines used Arras for about the same time as their HQs, and when we had day off duty we would go back there. We were dodging in and out of the line at different places for 3 or 4 months during 1917 till one day we entrained for Belgium in readiness for the Pashendale [sic] battle of October 1917, and found ourselves on the old familiar canal just left of Ypres again.

Dud English 15 inch shell Thiepval
September 1916

CHAPTER 13

The Third Battle of Ypres 1917

The plans were all made by the "brass hats" and we went into action between Bixhoote and Langemarke. Mud, mud, mud, ye Gods, I did not think there was so much mud in the world as there was in Belgium. The Somme had some mud, I'll own, but I think Belgium had the rest of the world's supply. We ate it, drank it, slept in it, and breathed in it for a fortnight or so while we were taking the ridge with the lines of "pill boxes" on it. [Pillboxes, I'd better explain were a lot of machine gun posts, which Fritz built. They were built of concrete and the walls were in some cases 4ft thick or more, but the walls at the rear were only about 2ft or less. So that when Fritz retired from them his guns gave them sacks with our troops in]. Some were larger than others and the one we claimed was about 12ft square. Fritz had hit the near one with shells a few times, so we hurried and built it up with the broken lumps of concrete and bricks from the ruins of Langemarke, which was about 500 yards on our left [what was left of it]. Here again it was useless to lay cable, so we had to use "Daylight Signalling Lamps" and flags. The country hereabouts is very flat and from the doorway of our pillbox we could see the shells bursting at night in Houthulst Forest, and the German guns a little farther back replying. So, of course, when we started using a lamp to send messages to some pillboxes up in front, Fritz started on us with some shells. He hammered us for an hour or more and several R.A.M.C. orderlies who happened to be passing at the time, dashed in for shelter.

Now I mentioned before that this pillbox was only about 12ft square, and in it were signallers, orderlies, some spare troops who were lost, and then these R.A.M.C. chaps came dashing in. Add to that the signalling equipment and a couple of stretchers and several chunks of concrete too big to move you can guess we had heaps of room, I don't think. Fritz

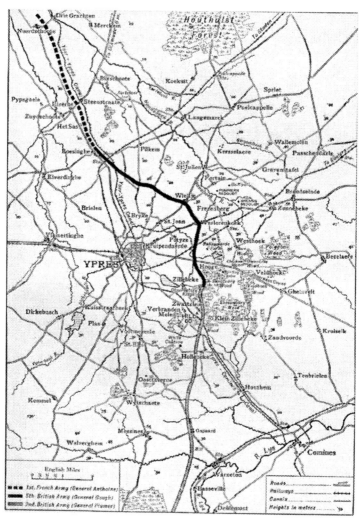

Ypres Salient before the battle of July 31st 1917

kept dropping shells all around the place, and we had one shell which as true as this diary is being written, hit the pillbox and stayed on top without bursting, and we climbed up and saw it laying there when the shelling had stopped. It was quite 3ft long and about 3 to 4ft round. As I say, we were packed in like sardines and, of course, as the RAMC lads had to stand near the doors there was absolutely no more room to stand a rifle upright, and suddenly a shell burst right in the doorway and took off

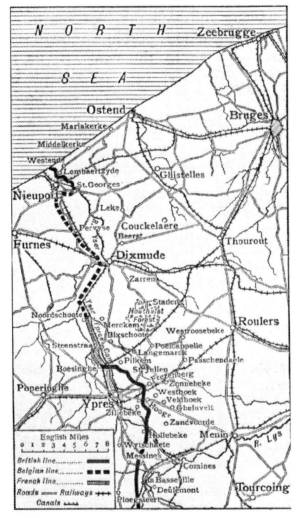

Ypres and around 1917

the arm of one of the RAMC lads as clean as though it had been done with a knife above the elbow. It only left a bit of flesh the thickness of my finger to hold it from falling to the ground. He screamed and lurched forwards and fell against a couple of pals covering them with his blood as his flesh flew all over us. I had a good splashing as I was standing just near the door round the corner, waiting for Fritz to stop shelling so that I could send a message.

Flanders mud

We tried to stop the blood for the poor devil but couldn't and to make it worse we could not lay him down, as there was no room. And then one of his pals did a thing that should have got him a dozen VCs. As I said, they were RAMC orderlies and knew how to set about stopping the blood but could not seem to do so, as the arm was off near the shoulder, so altho' Fritz was dropping shells thick and fast all over the place between our pillbox and Langemarke, a distance of 500 yards, this pal of the wounded one dashed right the way across to Langemarke through a proper inferno of fire to get a tourniquet to put on the wound to try to stop the blood. We watched him breathlessly, and swearing that he would never do it, also swearing to report it to the Brigade and see that he got his medal. We saw him fall at about 200 yards, roll over and over, and then up and gone again, with big shells falling all around him. I tell you he had a charmed life, for I'm sure he must have been severely blown over by some of the bursts. What saved him more than anything else was the mud. The shells would penetrate so far in the soft earth before bursting that a good deal of mud and water used to help drown some of the force of the explosion, and unless some shell happened to get you direct, you had a chance on the run. Still that does not detract one atom from the fact that he was doing as

*The English Infantry awaits the signal to attack in a trench fitted with
a gas trumpet alarm. Plugstreet Woods Jan 1917*

plucky a thing as was done over in France or Belgium, and he reached the
village what's more and then as a miracle the shelling stopped as suddenly
as a shower of summer rain does. Whether Fritz got tired or repented
[M'yes] we knew not, but that kid came trotting back across the shell holes
as white as a ghost except where his chum's blood had splashed him. As
the shelling had stopped some of the chaps got outside so that we could lay
the wounded one on the stretcher, and when we made him as comfortable
as possible we discovered the entrance to the pillbox was not wide enough
to let the stretcher pass out, so we had to stand him up again. He had some
grit too. He was conscious all the time, and when he stood up he grabbed
the leather strap of his steel helmet with his teeth. I was holding him round
his waist with his face close to mine and he murmured "Is my poor arm
right off?" but I said "Don't you worry Jock boy", and then he said he
would walk but, of course, we laid him gently on the stretcher outside the
pillbox and his pals carried him back to the first aid post. And I'm sorry to
say that other brave kid's dash through the barrage went for nothing as
they told us that the wounded one died at the first aid post through loss of
blood. Whether the other kid got a medal or not I don't know, but I heard

Remains of a German pillbox near Tyne Cot

the case being talked about at Brigade HQs some time after. If he never did get one he has always got the consolation of knowing that he did his bit towards saving his pal's life out there.

We lived in this pillbox for about a week enduring little hell for 23 hours out of 24, just because we used a flashlight I guess. Evidently Fritz didn't like signallers. And then we had a message up from Brigade to say we should be relieved that night. We were "relieved" in more senses than one believe me! One message I took while up there was to the effect that if our guns didn't lengthen the range or stop shelling altogether we should not have any troops left by morning, as they were they were dropping shells and killing our own men. The answer to that was that the guns were firing at extreme range, and could not advance a yard owing to the state of the ground, and I quite believe it from what I saw of the horses and gunners straining to get a gun out of a mud hole while on our way back. Well we got relieved at night, and although we were told we should have to come straight back to the canal bank the three of us faced it cheerfully although it was three miles. Two miles of that being across boggy country potted with shell holes full of slimy mud waiting for you to fall into at each step, and dressed as follows: British warm to keep out the cold, steel helmet to head off bits of shrapnel, gas helmets to keep out gas, rubber thigh boots to try to keep out the water but didn't, rifle to shoot someone but couldn't, ammunition ditto, haversack loaded, water bottle empty, field telephone, daylight signalling lamp, pair of flags, telescope, binoculars, helio and stand, bookcase for message pads, and several odds and ends including blanket and groundsheet. Just load yourself up with that lot reader and go for a walk across about 2 mile of waterlogged, shell holed Belgium, never knowing any moment whether a shell would come over and put you out of your misery, and then say if you think you are earning a 1/- per day. Perhaps you are saying "Alright don't cry about it, but get on with the story", so I'll do so.

We three lads did at last arrive at the old Yser Canal and after making a few enquiries, discovered HQs and found that the canal was well back out of range now and they could afford to be generous as regards fire. When we did arrive in the glow of the flames, the signal sergeant, who was not in the habit of throwing praise about had to admit that we certainly looked as tho' we had been through it, and I guess we did. We had each had a few falls in shell holes en route, and were simply caked with fawn coloured mud from the soles of our feet to our steel helmets, and looked as though we wanted soaking for a month. "Damn that, give us some grub" were our first words, and as we were the last lot to come in, our cook [as good a one as there was out there for looking after our "Mary" department, which accounted for the fact that we were very often used to collect round for him on pay days] told us we could eat and drink all that was left. I won't bore you with an account of our meal that night, but if you have ever seen three hungry pigs having their meal of pigs wash, then you've seen us feeding. However we could not hope to get any sleep for that night tired as we were, so we made the best of it sitting round the camp fire till daylight came and then went to the canal for an hours dig out. We were told to scrounge around for a dugout, as we should be there for two or three days, and we found some room in a well built "elephant dugout" for which I might say here and now I was grateful for, as we stayed there longer than expected, and on every night when it was a full moon Fritz's planes used to come over 10 or 12 at a time and do some awful damage amongst the troops that were in the corrugated Nissen Huts near the Canal. Also he dropped a bomb [it looked like an aerial torpedo], right between the ropes of a bell tent in which the Brigadier Major was sleeping just outside our dugouts. Fortunately it did not burst but it stood in the ground just where it fell with a frame of barbed wire around it, till someone from Ordnance came and took it apart. Had it burst we should have been entitled to another brand new Brigade Major. Fritz also used to drop them on the surrounding villages of Elverdinge and Vlamertinge, although there was not much of either of them left, but when in 1915 Fritz was always shelling them, a village between those two called Brilien used to get away almost scot free [I wonder why].

We were a week or ten days at this camp, and then went to Ypres with the Ramparts as Brigade HQs. I was at once detailed with 3 RE signallers to go to an outpost near the lakes of Zillebeke and Zonnebeke. I was in charge of this station at this time as although I was the youngest RE signaller [me having transferred to the RE signals by this time] I was the oldest soldier of the four or five of us by far, as the other three lads had only joined up since 1914, and my signalling days commenced in 1907- 08. I have only mentioned that fact for a reason I'll tell you of later, not for swank. Well now we took over the signal dugout from some "mob", I believe it was the Guards, and settled down for another week or so. I detailed off my three men to their various jobs, and put one on as operator straightway. Having ascertained that all lines were "through" to the various other posts and back to Brigade HQs, I took one of the lads round to inspect the trenches, which we were responsible for. That took 2 or 3 hours to do.

Gas Attack

Everything appeared satisfactory so we returned. Things were fairly "tame" about this time, just a few shells coming over now and then, or an occasional air scrap, but nothing to write home about. But one night when the wind was in Fritz's favour he let go a gas cloud, and as we were well up in the "Hoop" as it was called, it was difficult to get any proper information from the Battalion HQs as to the correct direction of the oncoming gas cloud, and it was essential for us to do so to enable us to transmit back to the Brigade, and they would tell the artillery where to drop a barrage of shells. There was a wildly exciting half an hour as there always was on an alarm of "Gas". Every other message that happened to be going anywhere at that time was sent [just as an SOS would be sent at sea], and the details as to the direction of the gas would follow as soon as possible. Evidently it was not coming through fast enough to suit

*A Somerset Light Infantry soldier in 1917
wearing a gas mask; by Sgt A Cornwell*

everybody, as our gas blanket, which hung over the door of all the dugouts to keep out the gas [perhaps] was wrenched to one side and a voice called "when are we going to get any news about this damned gas?" and, "Are you all asleep in here?" and a few more uncomplimentary things. Now I ask you reader, there was the operator straining every nerve to get the information that was so badly needed by all, but what he was not told he could not tell, and this blinding fool comes charging in cursing and raving at us. I let him rave for a minute, and then I said, "When we have something, you'll hear something, and not before, so get out and keep out". A remark that started a conversation something like this.

Him, "Do you know who I am?"

Myself, "No, and I don't care".

Him, "I'm the Sergeant Major of the East Lancs and I was a signal sergeant for 13 years".

Myself "I don't care if you are the SM of the Guards, and I've been a signal private for 11 years which is almost as good as your record".

Then I told him that as long as he had been a "Signal Sgt" all that time he should know one of the orders was that no unauthorised person has any right to be in or near a signals dugout, and that I should report him to Brigade HQ in the morning. He tried to put the wind up me by saying he wanted my name and number, which I gave him quick enough, but when he asked me who was in charge of the station, and found I was, he altered his tone. But after that, let me tell you that it was not him talking, but the rum issue. He had had more than his ration of rum. That was just a little pants to cheer us up, and nothing came of it, as I could make it rather warm for Mr Company Sergeant Major of the East Lancs. He said nothing and I didn't report him, so that was that.

The "gas" alarm "fizzed out" I'm glad to say, which was more than the one did earlier on the canal bank which I forgot to mention, so I will relate here what I saw of that one. At that time we were next to French troops who were on our left, and two pals and myself were detailed for a signal post between the British and French. We went to the dugout indicated and found we had to share it with two bearded Poilou's [French Tommies] who were also signallers. I could rattle off a bit of French lingo, and one of the "Froggies" could spit out a bit of "Anglais", so I had a fine old time with him for about a fortnight. We wrote to one another for sometime after we parted, till they suddenly stopped, so he may have got "fed up" or perhaps he got killed, which I sincerely hope was not the case, as he had a large family at home somewhere down the south of France. Well now, about this gas attack, Fritz sent it over one night thick and heavy, and we kept our gas masks on for hours. I can see the poor Froggie now spitting and spluttering and coughing as he was trying to speak a message over the phone to his troops. We had the sort of masks at that time that we had to pull right over our heads and tuck inside the necks of our khaki coats. Talk about stifling. The smell of those darned things were enough to gas us, without the real gas. The artillery promptly put down a barrage all along the front where the gas was coming from, and whether it was only meant to be a gas attack without an infantry to follow I don't know, or whether our artillery barrage made it too hot for him to leave his trenches, I don't know. Anyhow Fritz did not "come over" that time, and I must say this for the Artillery lads here, that they could put down a barrage when it was wanted. They whizzed over 18 pounders that night almost as fast as a machine gun could let rip bullets. It was grand to hear stream after stream of shells tearing into Fritz's trenches and that may have dampened any attempt of his to "come over" to pay our trenches a visit. But the unfortunate part of it was that the "gas cloud" came across just on relief night, that is, just when two battalions were being relieved by two from reserve. With the results that the trenches were packed with troops coming out and going in and they were mostly caught out of their dugouts and, of course, were unprepared.

Now just listen, reader, I expect the account of that little lot appeared in the papers over here something like this, the Germans launched a gas attack on the Western Front which failed before our fire. True enough, unless you read in between the lines. The German infantry attack, which may or may not have been intended, probably did fail, but the gas attack did not fail, and I'll now prove it to you. When things got normal again, and we could breathe freely once more, we took off our masks and made a few enquiries over the phones of how things were going on around us. We heard enough to convince us that all was not well, and when, as soon as dawn broke, we could see the Elverdinghe road back behind us, then we could tell what effect the gas attack had had. There was a constant stream of ambulances taking our gassed troops away as fast as the cars could load them, and how far through the night they had been doing the same thing we didn't know, but they were at it till late in the morning on that day. When I went down to Brigade HQs about 9am to get our days rations which we could not fetch overnight, I saw row after row of our lads lying on the ground and on stretchers waiting their turn to be taken to hospital. Some were dead, some just coughing their last spark of life out, but all were gassed. [And yet it was a failure in the press.] One good thing in Fritz's favour was this. The day broke and he put up a long line of observation balloons [sausages we called them], all along the line, so that he could see all these cars taking away the gassed troops, and had he been inclined he could have opened out with his guns and he could have killed hundreds more of our chaps, as the countryside all round was packed with troops of all sorts, but in the walk to the Brigade and back I did not even hear a rifle shot, let alone a shell. So although, as I said, the papers called it a failure, Fritz could see for himself that it was very successful from his point of view, which is all that mattered to him.

A dangerous shower

It was at this post, which was called "the liaison post" on account of British and French signallers working together, that my pal and I had to run stripped naked once to dodge the shell fire. I'll tell you about it. About 100 yards, as I said, from my dugout were a few trees more or less blown about by some heavy shells earlier in the war, and the ground around had some lovely big shell holes filled with water which had settled down and was fairly clean, as shell hole water went. One day

Tyne Cot Cemetery for British and Commonwealth troops

German Cemeteries on or near the Ypres Salient

Langemarck

"Grieving Parents" at Vladso near Ypres

while having a "scrounge around" I found an old trench pump which someone had dumped down, and I asked my pals to come and give me a hand and we would rig up a "shower bath" under one of the trees near the shell holes. We fixed it up all right by the cutting out the side of a petrol can, punching a hole in it, tying it up in the tree, and tying the rubber tube of the trench pump to it. One of us would stand under the shower and lather all over with soap while the other would pump, and then change over. The weather about this time was hot and sunny so we

had some enjoyable shower baths for a few days, till, of course, "nosey
parker" Fritz must "butt in". I suppose he got jealous because he hadn't
one like it. Anyhow one day we were out there having our usual shower
and splashing one another with this fairly clean water [there may have
been a few tadpoles and slugs pumped up but that didn't matter much],
when without any warning four whizz-bang shells came screaming at us
at about thousand miles an hour. Talk about nip to it; we didn't stop to
grab our clothes, but flew for our lives to the dug out, and I cut my knee
badly as I slipped down the steps. Didn't we curse Fritz when we got our
wind back. I suppose some darned Fritz observation officer was out
looking for something to shoot at when he spotted us two poor little
devils having our shower bath. No doubt we showed up fairly well
against the greenish background and the sun shining on our "glistening
bodies" made us too good for him to miss, but he did miss us, thanks
very much, and I'll bet he didn't half have a grin on his face when he saw
us do that sprint in the same sort of suit that Adam wore in the Garden,
only less. Later on we got our clothes thank you, as he only fired those
four shells, so they were made especially for us two. Two each. We sat
wrapped in blanket each till we were sure he wasn't going to shoot
again.

Now let me take you back to the dugout where I had the "conversation
with the SM of the "Lancs." I forgot to mention that I had no idea at all
that he was a Sgt Major when he pulled our gas blanket aside and poked
his head in, as I could not see his arms with the brass crown on it, denoting
his rank until he was told by me to get out and keep out. Instead of going
out he came in in a blustering sort of way which most Sgt Majors have
[and some of them are only ten a penny], all made to stand up, and then I
could see his rank. It was after I saw who he was that we had the
conversation. Well that's enough about him.

So I'll get on with the agony. Poor old Fowler, who I referred to earlier,
was on this station with me, and him and I went out one night to repair a
line which could not be reached by daylight on account of those
unpleasant neighbours of ours from Germany. So it had to be done in the
"silent hours of the night". We found the break without too much
trouble, and repaired it, and everything was all over bar the shouting. But,
as it was a rather "peaceful" sort of night we sat down in a shell hole, kept
low, and had a smoke, and then sat and watched the "Very Lights" and

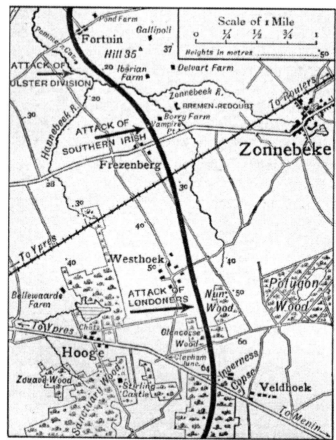

The Battle area East of Ypres, showing line before attack on August 16 1917

Star Shells going up all round us. I am only mentioning this just to show you that being in the Salient at night with all the lights going up, made it appear as though Fritz was in a complete circle around us, and we were cut off. 'Twas a funny sensation.

About a month was spent by us up there and the usual message came through that we were being relieved in a day or two. In time we were relieved, and at 2 AM one morning I have a distinct recollection of cycling past the ruins of the Cloth Hall in company with about a dozen more chums on my way to Wormhoudt, about 12 or 14 miles I believe; may be more, I forget now, but if the reader had a map of Belgium, just look up Ypres to Wormhoudt and sort it out. We got there near about dawn, [as

Flooded trench and bunker in Plugstreet Woods January 1917. The English High Command took these special conditions into account by issuing troops with rubber kit

This is where the modern war machine raged. The battlefield near Paschendaele 1917

there were no estaminets open en route I guess], and, of course, had to wait for the wagons to come before we could get any breakfast, so we sat about doing nothing while billets were being arranged and looked out. The Brigade HQs were billeted in a private racing stable in the hayloft and 'twas very comfortable while it lasted.

CHAPTER 14

Return to Arras

The next day we entrained again for Arras and went to Dainville for a few days, a village just behind Arras. From there we went into action just under the hill from Monchy-le-Preux again about 399 yards to the right of the river Scarpe. Just below us were the railway and a level crossing where "in former times "a red brick signal box had stood. But of course Mr Fritz had undertaken the contract for demolishing it [without permission]. The bricks, I might tell you, came in very useful to us for making a first class field oven in the side of the trench which we were now living in, and we used to have some champion bread-puddings for dinner, with "Tommy Ticklers"[32] celebrated "Red Plum jam". If ever I met "Mr Tommy Tickler" I'm going to ask him why, wherefore, and what not, was it that our Brigade HQs was always getting "Red Plum jam". [I cannot walk by a red plum jam tree now without trembling for fear it is going to fall on me]. Did I say always had it, by mistake one day we had some Marmalade and I saw a "Jock " eating it for breakfast. Now as I was not very acquainted with such high living, I asked him what it was like. Having received a satisfactory reply between the bites I decided to try it, and I'm pleased to say that an Englishman can eat "marm" on toast just as well as a "Jock".

Off we go again. The usual old routine, operating linesman, and any other spare job that came along. These having been completed to the satisfaction of "Duggie Haig" and his followers for a few weeks, we were allowed to lose ourselves in the village of Warhus, which is on a hill some distance from Arras.

Brief Leave

Just at that time, my turn came for leave to England again [end of January

1918] so I went to Arras one night and caught the leave train. I won't bore you with details of the trip to the boat, as I would sooner forget it, only to say there was no improvement since 1915 as regards leave trains. Please don't think I wanted a first class carriage with cushions, and roses round the door, only a lady would expect that, and we had no ladies "out there", [with the exception of the Red Cross nurses who were ladies in every sense of the word, from the soles of their feet to the crowns of their heads], and I can rough it with any as regards hardships, but a joke is a joke, and I think the leave trains were the standing jokes of the war. By the way I got 24 hours absent on that leave. It doesn't matter what it was for, altho' I know, of course, and I got back to France after about 10 or 12 days leave and found them still at Warhus. Of course I was for the "high jump", but when I explained the "situation" truthfully to the officer i/c he gave me a "wash out" [not a wash house] which meant no punishment. We had several signalling schemes while at rest at Warhus and then moved right up into the action to relieve the Guards who had been in the line 6 weeks and were taking over our village for a six week rest. Fritz cancelled that by attacking the other side of the Scarpe, and we heard that the Guards had been rushed up there after about a week of rest. Sorry for 'em.

Death of Fowler

Now our HQs was in a trench named "Pudden Trench", quite near the villages of Fampoux, Gavrelle and Oppy, and they say the barbed wire defending Fritz's trenches was over 50 yards deep. 'Twas here where my old pal Fowler was killed by a piece of shrapnel going down through his shoulder and out near his heart. He knew he had come to the end of the war for him too, because he said so. He said, "It's alright I've finished". 'Twas rather a funny way he was killed all owing to mistake. It appears we had two cables running from Brigade HQs to Battalion HQs but in different directions, but coming round to meet again at the Battalion HQs. They were laid across country like that to try and avoid some of the shellfire, and one day the signal corporal yelled, " next out quick, the line to the battalion has gone". Without stopping to see which of the two lines that was bust Fowler grabs a field-phone and some cable and dashes off along the first line he picked up. And he dashed to his death. Fritz sent over a salvo for something to do just at that minute into the village of Fampoux near us, and as he, Fowler, ran, a piece of the shell got him as I said. As it turned out he was on the wrong cable, and had he taken the other which I had grabbed and set out on he would have been alright, as I did not have a shell fall within a 100 yards of me all the way out and back. I found the break and repaired it, and it was only when I got back that I heard that he was dead. My luck was in that time.

Night Barrage

Some time after, a corporal and myself got trapped in a sunken road alone nearly all the night and dare not poke our nose up. It was the same line again, and it started like this. The corporal was told to take one man [he took me], and go along the line running across the country to the left battalion and drag it for safety into a newly dug trench which was running in the same way. The trench had only been dug a couple of nights before, and was a good deep one. Anyone knows the more you dig down the more soil comes up to put on the sides, so, of course this trench was very noticeable to Fritz, but he had left it alone up to that time. Of course it was in full view by day, and Fritz could easily see if many troops passed up and down by day, so he naturally thought it was being used at night, and just because that night was the one we were sent out to do the job he must choose the same night to wipe that trench off the map. And he did too. [I've often thought since that that night was the means of my start for Pleurisy.] We were told to start after tea, and by the time we reached the trench where it crossed the sunken road it would be dark enough to get the cable and peg it all along the side of the trench to the Battalion HQs. That sounds easy on paper and it would have been easy on "manoeuvres". "Out there" was another story. Anyhow after tea the corporal "Skin" and I started out. He was nicknamed "Skin" because that's about all he was made of and a few odd bones. However we set out and had about 2 miles to go. The first half-mile was easy as we simple had to hold the cable in our hands to guide us. We had no trench to put that in, but when we got over the brow of the hill the trench began, and we started dragging in the cable and pegging it up as ordered. Now, of course, had it been daylight we should have been in full view of Fritz, and should not have stayed there long. "Skin" being the tallest was down in the trench pegging it up quite nicely all the way along, and I was out over the top picking it up and unhitching it from different things I stumbled over in the dark, but did not know till next morning that some were dead bodies of troops, but I'll tell you of that later. We reached the sunken road and found the trench on the other side as indicated, and laid the cable into the road and then into the trench, and carried on all the way up to the Battalion HQs. In some places the cable was 2 or 3 hundred yards from the trench. On arrival, and after trying out our instrument on the line and finding everything was alright and the line was in working order, we set off back.

Now a job just as I've described is not done in five minutes, so I reckon it was somewhere near 10 pm when we started back, and we came all the way along the trench so as not to lose ourselves, not because we were frightened of shell fire, as it was all quiet as a grave, a proper peaceful night, and I was just thinking that Fritz was behaving himself like proper "little gent" [the calm before the storm]. "Skin" and I trudged along the trench one behind the other, talking and having a fag till I reckoned we were within a stone's throw of the sunken road, when with a roar and a bang a big cloud of earth went up to heaven just ahead of us. "Skin" said something like "Blimey kid that was a near 'un"; I agreed it was too darn near to be healthy. It was a lucky job we were in the trench instead of walking along the top, or I may not be writing this. We thought it was only a "stray one" that had "broke loose" from somewhere, and after getting our temperatures back to normal, we agreed to step out a bit quicker before another may wander over looking for someone to "smash up". As I said just now we thought we were within a stone's throw of the sunken road just as the shell came over, but it just shows how anyone can get deceived as to the distance at night. So we "stepped out" and I'll swear someone must have moved that sunken road while our backs were turned as I thought we were never coming to it. Another blinding flash and several unearthly bangs suddenly shook the earth all round us, and "Skin" yelled, "run". I needed no second bidding, but I didn't run, "I flew". Heads down away both of us dashed hell for leather up that winding trench till we suddenly came around one of the bends and out into the sunken road. "Skin" suggested stopping to get our wind back a minute, and I was certainly agreeable as I had a lot to get back. So we crouched down close to the bank nearest the enemy for a breather, as we fondly imagined, for a few minutes. Little did we dream that we should have to stay there for the rest of the night, wondering just how long it would be before a shell should put us "out of mess". Fritz seemed to have got an idea in his head that the newly dug trench was going to be filled with passing troops that night, but he was quite wrong as no-one at all went along it, and if they had tried to do so it would have been their grave. As I said, we crouched by the bank in the roadside, and then Fritz really started in earnest. He dropped shells with the regularity of a clock ticking all over the trench from one end to the other from about midnight till just before dawn. First he would send over a salvo of four just over the hill towards Brigade on the trench, then he would lower his sights on his guns and come back 100 yards or so. Up and down that trench with remarkable rapidity considering the size of shells he was using. You could have put a donkey and cart in any one of the shell holes he made. "Skin" and myself never expected to see daylight any more, "honest Injun". Sometimes Fritz would drop them on the sunken road and the ground would heave and tremble all around us. The banks of the road were not a bit more than 10 ft high and sloping at the top, so we had nothing to crawl under, and the lumps of earth would fall on us and around us like rain. Reader you may be saying to yourself "Well, you must have been fools to stay there". Believe me we should have been fools to stay there had there been anywhere else to go, but when shells are falling here, there, and everywhere every minute or so, and you don't know where the next lot is coming, and they are coming over 4, 6, or 8 at a time all over the place in the middle of the night, and couple that with the fact that we did no know any other way back to Battalion HQs except by way of the trench where Fritz was dropping 'em. Also we were out there as linesmen that night and our orders were to get that line through. There were no dugouts of any sort just where we were, so all we could do was to stick it and hope for the best. The "best" kept us where we were until dawn. Once during the night Fritz eased up a little, and we dashed up and "tapped in" a cable and found we could speak through to Brigade HQ, but we did not expect to speak to Battalion HQs although we tried it. We just had time to tell Brigade that we were alive and kicking so far, and to answer their enquiries as to where all the shells were dropping that they could hear at Brigade; also to tell them that we expected the cable between us and the Battalion HQ's was "blown to blazes" [only more so] and to get the "joyful" order to get it through before we came in, when Fritz opened up again, and his very first salvo nearly did for us.

We did not quite finish saying all the "complementary" things to Brigade that we had intended to say, before we had to snatch up our instruments and fly for our lives about 100 yards down the sunken road again, for safety. If those at Brigade HQs only knew one quarter of the names that

"Skin" and I called 'em, they would have gone straight over to Fritz and have given themselves up to him. So you see, that order from Brigade HQs and the fact that we did not know of any "Better 'ole" to go to, explains the reason why we were fools to stay there. So there we stayed saying our prayers one minute, and cursing the next, if one dropped a bit too near to be pleasant. If ever I longed for daylight before in my life, I did that night. At last we could see a thin streak of light breaking over behind Fritz's lines, and then, and not till then, did Fritz stop shelling. The only consolation we had as regards weather was that it was fine but bitterly cold out there waiting for dawn. Before it was properly light "Skin" and I moved off after giving our frozen feet and hands a good stamping and banging, and made for the trench again. What a mess! There wasn't any trench there but just a long line of broken country where the trench had been. Fritz had simply pumped shells all the way up and down till there was not 10 yards of that trench that was any good, so what hopes for our cable there?

We stumbled along in and out of the shell holes in the mist of dawn, without any fear of being seen by Fritz since there was a low mist hanging over the whole country around us. We found that it was useless to go up the "trench" as it needed new cable for the whole length of it, from the Battalion HQs nearly back to the sunken road. So "Skin" decided to come back to the sunken road, "tap in" on the cable and tell Brigade all about it. On the way we saw several dead bodies of "Jocks" lying around all bloated and turned black, and I saw the lower part of a "Jock's" leg in a shell hole.

We arrived back at Brigade HQs and had breakfast with a bit extra for luck, and our tot of rum kept for us from the overnight issue, as, remember, we had been out from soon after tea, and the rations had not arrived when we set out the night before. Well, after a good feed, a lot of rum, and a couple of the inevitable fags, "Skin" and I set out again with a small drum of cable to put the line through, or bust, from the sunken road to Battalion HQs. By now, of course, it was broad daylight and we had to keep to the trench this side of the sunken road, not on top like we could in the dark. We arrived at first break in the cable and made a joint, and then started reeling out the new cable off the drum we carried, laying it in and out of the long line of shell holes which used to be the trench, but now wasn't. Fritz could now see us and we were "sniped at" several times from the direction of the railway bank that Fritz held. As long as he did not shell us we did not mind so much as we were moving along all the time and it would have taken a very lucky bullet [or unlucky for us] to have got us bobbing up and down among the shell holes. But shelling was different; the darned things would have finished us off.

Aerial Combat

As we were reeling the cable out, stumbling along, cursing at Fritz and laughing in turns, we heard the hum of an aeroplane over our heads and we knew it was one of ours without needing to look up, as all troops who had been "out there" any considerable time could easily distinguish the sounds of the planes engines, so we carried on. Soon we heard a different tune, and looking up we saw four of Fritz's planes coming over. They were painted in all sorts of weird designs, and as they drew nearer, one left the rest and dived down on the single plane of ours and fired his machine gun at him. "Skin" and I sat down in the shell holes and forgot about our cable-laying job for a little while, in the excitement of watching this thrilling "scrap" not more than 500 or 600 ft in the air above us. Our plane was one of those slow flying things that used to get on the troops nerves by flying or "crawling", up and down the lines just behind our front line trenches all day long "observing". But the four Fritz planes were a part of that "Circus Squadron" which used to appear so much in the press. We could see that our "old" plane was doomed from the start, as Fritz kept flying over him all the time and pumped bullets at him at every swerve. Some of them fell all around us once, and old "Skin" gave a yelp once as several hit the dust just behind his back. Our plane did the only thing it was possible for him to do, viz, "keep on walking", or rather flying, till he was well down near the ground, but it was no use, as Fritz hung on to him all the way down, and fired his machine gun at every opportunity. We could see the enemy pilot peering over the side of his plane as he kept diving at our poor devil, and the front of Fritz's plane was painted to represent a monster shark with big red teeth and eyes at the side of the body of the plane. It was enough to put "the wind up" any uncivilised savages, but I don't think all the planes in "the Fatherland" would have put the wind up our airman. However our plane was driven lower and lower till it finally hit the ground nice and steady about 400 yards from us. The undercarriage sunk into the soft earth, and the wings crumpled up, but the planes body kept perfectly upright. Fritz was now about 200ft up and well behind our lines. When the lad in the trenches in front saw our plane was down, every one opened up rifle and machine gun fire all around. I hoped he would be brought down, although he deserved to get away with it, which he did. I reckon there was a thousand rounds fired at him just as he started to climb again, and I expected to see him riddled but he kept climbing and swerving all the way up over out of the way, and finally flew out of range. Giving credit where it's due I should say he earned an "Iron Cross". It was a sight worth going all through the war to see.

After he had fled, "Skin" and I turned our attention to our plane lying so forlorn where it had fallen. I said to "Skin" "I'll bet they are both dead after that lot". "Skin" answered something like "Ah to be sure". There was no movement at all to be seen, so I said "Let's nip across to it", but as we could see it was in the direction of the Brigade HQ that we were making for, but a bit to the left, we decided to lay the cable as far as possible up the line of shell holes and then up across the 100 yards or so of open country, as we were in full view of Fritz's snipers don't forget. So that's what we started to do. We kept one eye on the plane, one on the job we were doing, and the "weather eye" on Mr Fritz, but as we stumbled along I saw an arm waving from the plane. He could, of course, see "Skin" and me stumbling along and was trying to attract our attention. So I knelt and waved back at him. Then he raised his head out of the cockpit and called "Whereabouts are we, boy?" I explained as well as I could, and asked if he wanted any help, but as Fritz was watching his little business and started sniping at us and him, he yelled back "No don't come over I'll manage". He got down into the body of the plane again and in a moment or so bobbed up again and his pal was with him. Then he asked which was the best side to jump out of the plane. We yelled back "Where you are now" as the side of the plane luckily faced our lines. So he climbed out of the plane to the ground, helped his pal out who was wounded, and put his pal's arm around his neck and started walking towards us. Between them and us there was a dip in the ground, but as soon as they left the side of the plane the dammed snipers fired two or three rounds at them, and made them separate and run into the dip. We could see that one was wounded and limping badly, so the darned snipers must have seen it too, as they had glasses no doubt. When these two ran down into the dip we thought perhaps the snipers had hit them again, so "Skin" said "Come on kid, chance it" and we sprang out of the shell holes and ran towards them. But we found there was a bit of a trench in the dip, and some of our troops in it and as we topped the rise we saw them both being lifted down into the trench safe. Then we scooted back quick to the cable laying. We got through at last to the Battalion HQs, and put the line right and told them all about the air fight and what a lovely view we had had of it, and all that, thank you. We answered the question "Were the blokes killed?" about 50 times, had a chat with a few old pals and set off back to Brigade HQs getting there about a couple of hours before dinner. So old "Skin" and I returned after a glorious "night out". 'Twas all included in the war I suppose, and taking things as they came, we had some very rough times, also some very smooth times, and I only heard the remark passed once out there that someone didn't give a damn that even if a certain thing belonged to King George, he wasn't going to give it away.

Comic relief

It was rather amusing so I'll tell you about it. We were "on vacation" at the time, having a bit of a rest back in a nice little French village behind the lines. The weather was rotten, the dinner was rotten, the blinking Field Cashier was rotten as he could not be found and we were broke, the transport was rotten because it had not arrived with the mail, the rotten war was rotten, the whole world was rotten just about that time, so, of course, everyone's temper was on edge. It was one of those periods, which occurred sometimes when everything was against one. We had 'em like that you know, the sort of feeling when you feel as though you would like to load your rifle and blow your blasted head off if it wasn't for the mess on the nice "clean" billet floor. Or the sheets we didn't sleep in. However about this "King George" job. We had just been served "dinner", and either the cook was rotten for once, or else his clever hand had failed him for once, but the "dinner" that day was not what you would like to offer a lady if you took her out for the evening [unless she was a char lady], and we had a chap of the "Lancs." attached to us as orderly. He had his "dinner" in his canteen and placed it on the ground to go and "scrounge" a chunk of bread to help "fill up", and as soon as he turned his back a dog walked in at the door of the barn, where we were "in residence" as they say "higher up", [only we "flew no flag"], and started lapping up some of the "gippo", [gravy] of which the said dinner was composed [in fact 'twas more "gippo" than dinner that day, so who could blame a dog for being mistaken]. When he turned around and saw the dog lapping his "dinner" he picked up the iron camp kettle and flung it at him, to catch the poor old tyke such a smack as to bring his breakfast up, if he had any. An old French woman who was watching the lions fed, [us], yelled something at the orderly and he politely said "Oui Madame", meaning "Yes Missus", as the British Tommies usually said "Oui Madame" to any question out of politeness. But "Oui Madame" was apparently not the correct thing to say at that time, as it appears she said to him "Here that's my dog, and would you now like me to throw that tin at you," and, of course, he had said "Oui Madame", and the old lady promptly took him at his word and threw it at him. It was a proper "panto" whilst it lasted, and I thought there would be a couple of murders done in a minute or so to liven things up a bit. Of course the French language not being the orderly's strong point, one of the other chaps had interpreted the old French woman's question for him, and then he caused roars of laughter by saying "Missus I don't care a damn [only more so] if it's King George's dog, he ain't "mucking in" [Sharing] my dinner." It was proper prolonged by the old lady saying "Oui monsieur" and she did not know what he had said to her. It was just the sort of comedy at the right time to take some of the rotten feelings away. Many little "pantos" such as that were constantly occurring in different places to keep our tails up.

More air aces

While I was writing about the aeroplanes a German airman reminded just now me of another daring bit of flying. Please let me say, in passing, that I do not want you to think I'm sticking up for German airman in preference to ours, as I'm only writing what I actually saw or did, and any daring things done by our airmen usually took place behind the German lines where Fritz usually took good care to keep in daytime. Maybe there is a Hun back somewhere in Germany who is, perhaps, opening up his diary and who will, perhaps have some of the deeds of our airmen to record what occurred behind their lines. Well now, the other particularly daring bit of flying was done one evening just as everyone had about finished their tea and was sitting about smoking. Just between Arras and Lens was very long line of Kite balloons of ours floating gaily up in the air with the occupants keeping a watchful eye, [or otherwise], on the movements of Fritz behind the German lines. I suppose they were roughly half a mile apart at various heights, when suddenly a small but very fast Fritz plane seemed to drop from the sky and fire about a dozen incendiary bullets into one that immediately burst into flames and dropped. He then flew perfectly level at the next and repeated the dose, and on again to number three with the same telling effect and again to numbers four and five. To make perfectly sure, and I won't say more than that, but before our very eyes as we stood there gazing up, we saw at least 5 balloons go down in flames. These balloons, for those who are not in the know, were anchored at least $2^1/_2$ to 3 miles behind our front line and not "too high up", so that Fritz had to come well over and well down to get at them. While he was among the balloons tearing along the line between them at their own height, of course our guns dare not fire as I believe our observers jumped with their parachutes when he started on them. So our guns might have killed them as they floated down had they fired. But when he had finished the job and had turned to fly back to his own lines, all the guns in the neighbourhood that could be brought to bear were turned loose at him, but he sailed serenely along as though they were throwing stones at him, and he simply kept at the same level he was at when he fired at the balloons, not half a mile up, and flew home.

More than one Tommy said that they admired his pluck and that he deserved to get away with it, and I agree that he did, although we cursed the gunners for rotten shooting of course and told some of them that they couldn't hit a house tied to the muzzle of their guns.

CHAPTER 15

March 1918

Well now, after the usual spell up, we came back for a bit of rest to the village of Blagny just in front of Arras, and were billeted near an RAMC dressing station in the grounds of a big "one time" chateau. There were some grand artificial lakes in the grounds around which we used to bathe in between the times of Fritz's shelling which occurred daily whenever he felt like "strafing" someone. After about a fortnight of this we were once more taken up to the same place again, "Pudden Trench".

We are now at the beginning of March 1918 and still going strong but about this time, of course you all know now, Fritz must have been preparing things for his last desperate gamble, viz the big offensive of 1918. So it was a very lively shop up in the front of Arras roundabout March and April 1918 believe me. As time drew on towards the end of March we had orders one day for all our blankets and ground sheets, and our packs and all superfluous kit to be packed and taken back to the transport lines when the wagon came up at night. We packed up as ordered, and were then left with just "fighting orders" which, for the benefit of the uninformed, I'll explain; this meant rifle and bayonet, ammunition, haversack, water bottle and straps, steel helmet and gas bags. Now let me tell you, the nights were bitter cold with hard white frosts every morning, and getting the order "umpteen times" every night to "stand to" and "man the trenches", naturally didn't improve our health. Every morning before dawn we could be seen "standing to" in the trench waiting for Fritz's "big push" that we knew was coming, but not when. I'll explain here that from the part of the trench which a few pals and myself were detailed to hold we had a clear view across the River Scarpe [which at this point was only about 30 yards wide] of the hills running away up to Monchy, and when the attack did come on, I believe, March 23rd, we could see Fritz strolling along in

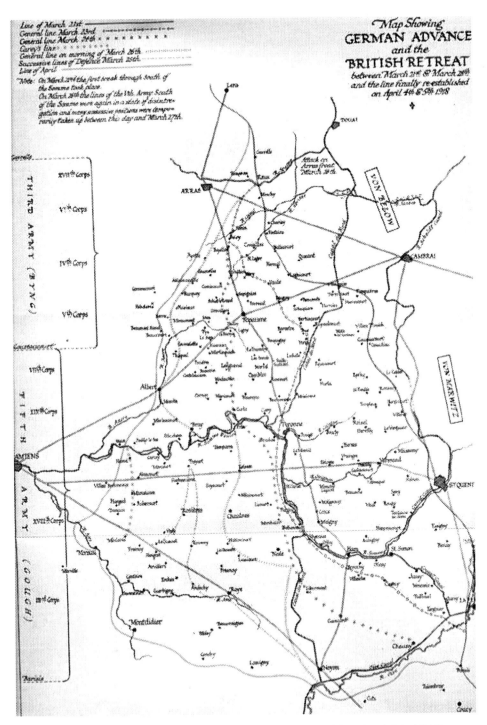

The German advance and the Allied retreat; March 21st–April 5th 1918

extended order all along the hillside. But we had orders for some reason or other, not to fire at them, whereas if we could have been allowed to open fire we could have killed heaps. It appears that the Scarpe was the northern limit of the "push", and directly to our front was not attacked although we were, of course, subjected to heavy shelling all the time, to keep us in order, I guess. As long as Fritz did not "come over" direct in our front we were not to give the game away as to whether our trenches were occupied or evacuated. At least that's how we took it, so I suppose there was something in it, and, of course, we obeyed orders, which is wise on active service [sometimes], and did not shoot, but had the mortification of seeing old Fritz's troops roaming about as they liked in what used to be our land a short time ago. We could see our old Brigade HQ where we used to make the "bread pudden", burning across the river, as those in occupation had fired it before they retired, and I remember someone saying at the time "Run across somebody and tell old Fritz not to blow up our oven". What hopes. Of course our artillery were not letting Fritz have it all his own way, only they were firing at those at the top of the hill around Monchy, and the Fritzs on the lower parts were having a day off. We were held just as we stood in readiness for two or three days, and then had orders to clear out quick and get back to the railway bank a little further in the rear known as the "Triangle", a junction where the lines parted for Lens. We took up position on the bank for a couple of days and it was here that I began feeling the effects of the weather. We all had caught bad colds, and no wonder, and after two or three days on the railway bank where I suffered agonies, we dropped back to some old German artillery dugouts which were used prior to the Easter Monday battle of Arras 1917. I was warned off as operator in one of the dugouts, and used to have to sleep on the steps of it when I was off duty. We had no groundsheets or greatcoats so you can guess how we "slept". I used to sit huddled up coughing and barking all day and night with a pain just under my ribs on the right side which felt as if my ribs had become interlocked one over the other. I stood this pain for several days till I could stick it no more and our officer asked me one day what the matter was. I told him and he went straight away and brought back a Medical Officer pal of his. They were both good sports. The MO said "What's up laddie?" and again I explained. He told me to get my coat off and open my shirt, and then he started tapping all over the chest till he came to a spot, which made me yelp. Then he said "Pleurisy". I, of course, was just as wise then as I was before, and I thought he was swearing at me for yelping. Then he said "He will have to go to hospital at once". My own officer said he did not want to lose me as I was a useful chap, always willing and a few more nice things which I won't bore you with, and could it be arranged for me to go back to an RAMC camp, and pick up again, as he thought that if I got to hospital I might get sent elsewhere when I recovered. For my part I did not want to go, as I had visions of going down to the Base hospital somewhere for a month, and then get well again and be sent to some other "mob" amongst a lot of strangers, and I did not want to leave all my old pals who I had been with for so long. But the MO said "All that I can do is to make out a sick report, and the rest is up to chance once he leaves here".

CHAPTER 16

Pleurisy

So I was told to keep myself as warm as possible and to go back with the ration wagon, which came up each night; some job on to keep yourself warm out there about that time. Well the wagon arrived after dark, and I was bundled into the limber part and wrapped some bread sacks around me. I was taken to a first aid post somewhere amongst the ruins of Arras, and my first dose of medicine at the hands of the RAMC was a basin of cocoa. I was given that and told to take off my putties and wrap up in a pile of blankets to wait for the "convoy". I suppose I went to sleep, for the next I know was that I was on a stretcher in a motor ambulance going along some French road through the night. Where I was or where I was going I neither knew or cared. We pulled up at some big clearing station somewhere and I was lifted and carried into a long hut, which was packed with wounded and sick of all regiments. There particulars were taken again, and I was once more left alone to wait for the ambulance car again to take me to the Red Cross train this time. I began to think I was right for a spell in hospital at the Base for a month at least, but I had a bigger surprise than that later on. I might mention here that all men who had served at the "Battle of Mons" were wearing a Mons ribbon[34] at this stage of the war, and I was wearing my tattered bit of a medal ribbon. I only mention that to show you how I found favour at the hands of the American Red Cross people.

Well now, when the train [see end note pages 184–185] had arrived at this clearing station and all "walking cases" were told to "fall in" outside the hut, I said to an orderly standing near me, "Here chummy I can walk you know". He looked at my medical card and saw I had Pleurisy. Then he said, "Pop your boots on or you might not get away for a day or two". So I took his tip and "fell in" with all the others, as I didn't like lying about on stretchers. We eventually got away and after a long train ride with a motor ambulance ride at the other end, we arrived at Étaples on the coast, and I at last arrived at a big American hospital there. At least Americans seemed to be in charge everywhere. I went to a marquee fitted up as a hospital ward and had a change of underclothes, a bath and a feed, and was told the Major would see us shortly.

Well now, I'll show you how my bit of Mons medal ribbon answered a lot of questions for me. As I said, it was all American orderlies and officers knocking about here, and the orderly who took my particulars said to me "What dirty old bit of ribbon is that you're wearing guy?" I answered "Mons, chummy, ever heard of it?", as I thought that by being American he might not have heard of Mons, as they were three years late coming into the war. So he said "Look here bo' I've got to enter all the particulars of everyone who enters this ward, so let's get wise to your case." So I answered all questions he put to me and when he came to "what service"? I said 12 years, he looked up and said is that right? I said "nearly". Then he said "Service in France". I said I came out in 1914. Then he said "Bo'! How d'you like to slip across to the United Kingdom?" I told him to ask me another. "Well," he said, "Don't go too far from this marquee, as the old guy of a Major will be round any old time, and I'll stuff in a word for you". I shook hands with that Yankee orderly [and myself]. I hung around as ordered and some time during the evening the old American Major came in and inspected me thoroughly. When he had finished he entered some more particulars on my medical card, which all wounded and sick Tommies carried around with them, and then he said "Well boy I've booked you for the UK, see there". I looked on my card and saw he had written HSC. I asked him what that meant and he said "Hospital Ship, Cabin". I said "Thank you Sir!" believe me. Well at about 2am or maybe 3am, I was awakened from my dreams in the cosiest bed I had slept in for many a day, and had some cocoa and buttered rolls given me, and was told to get up and get ready for a car ride. I got into the ambulance with others, went down to the train, on the boat at Boulogne and across to Dover. We entrained again and found we were en route for good old Plymouth. I got there sometime, somehow, someday, early in April 1918, and went to an infant's school at Camels Head, Devonport. I was told to go to bed and have a sleep after more cocoa and bread rolls. Of course we had a few feeds en route at different times and places. I stayed there a month and then transferred to the Military Drill Hall near Millbay station as a convalescence case. May and June were the loveliest months I have ever experienced at Plymouth. I was getting fit again now, and was allowed out, almost as freely as we wished. 'Twas a VAD hospital at Millbay as far as I recollect, and the nurses they were nurses, ladies and mothers combined. They were the finest bunch of ladies any troops could wish to be among. Nothing was too much trouble for them to do for one, and any little thing you may want brought from town they would bring in when they were off duty, not only at Millbay but at Camels Head as well. I did not have too much "hospital service" considering the nature of my complaint, which took time, as the officer pointed out each morning when I asked him to mark me "out". For the time I did have I must say that all the trained nurses, VADs or otherwise, that I had the pleasure to be under, were the finest bunch of ladies I wish to meet, and I take my hat off to them.

I never was one who wanted to be "lying idle" if I could be doing something, so although the conditions of life at Millbay hospital were everything any reasonable person could wish for [unless he was unnatural and could never be satisfied], I was feeling quite fit and well again, so I used to peg away at the old medical officer every morning he used to come round, and asked him to get me away on leave and then rejoin my unit somewhere, till eventually he did give in one morning to a certain extent. [I believe my Mons medal ribbon was something to do with it again by what the old boy said.] However it appears that Millbay had to clear out some of their patients to make room for more, and the old MO said this day "You have been asking for some time to be marked out haven't you?" I said I had. "Well," he said, "the reason I have not done it before is because these ladies say you are such a willing chap at washing up and helping the wards etc etc, that they don't wish you to go". I had no idea that I had been so useful to them, altho' I own I certainly did volunteer to wash up after meals every day for about 80 patients, but perhaps that was because I had my eye on a big dinner [and they could cook, mind, these ladies]. Anyway I told the old MO, who was a real old father by the way, that I had not enlisted to be a regular "washed up", altho' I did not mind helping at all. So it finished up by my being sent back with a few more to Camels Head as the old MO said "If I mark you furlough, you'll probably get a months leave, and be out of there again in another week or so after, and according to your ribbon you have done

The knee deep morasse near Paschendaele made the rescue of wounded difficult

your bit". I thought it was very nice of the old boy, but I felt just like a big blubbering school kid when he gets his Sunday School prize and gets a pat on the head from his teacher for being such a good boy, and all that sort of "slop". [Reader I've had some of that, so I know what I'm talking about.]

CHAPTER 17

Demobilisation and Armistice

Anyhow I told the old cook that I didn't mind going back "out there" as I had heaps of pals there yet. But he would not have any and I went as I said, to Camels Head again. Of course now we were out of "hospital blue", thank the Lord, for if ever troops were dressed up as "guys" they were when they donned "hospital blue", and we had our khaki back again. We all had new suits served out and were allocated out till 9pm. I stuck it at the Camels Head hospital for a fortnight and then got leave for 10 days and orders to proceed to the Command Depot at Thetford in Norfolk where I arrived sometime in July 1918.

Thetford is, I should say, alright if you have "tons of money" and nothing to do but stroll shooting pheasants and partridges, but as for keeping troops up on the hill top in a camp, 'ugh, I sooner rather have been sent to Dartmoor. [I've been to Dartmoor reader, not at "His Majesty's request" though mind, but away in 1908. I had the doubtful pleasure of marching from Plymouth to Salisbury Plain and we passed Princeton at Dartmoor en route]. Well I stayed at Thetford Command Depot for a couple of months, and to get away from the darned place I entered my name for a course of "physical training" which was to last a month, and seven days leave for all who passed, and then rejoin our own depots. I passed alright, had my seven days leave and orders to join the Royal Engineers Signal Depot at Bedford. So I arrived at Bedford in September 1918. Bedford I might say was more civilised than Thetford. In fact the troops there were "quite tame". There were a very choice selection of Australian and New Zealand Tommies attached to the Signal Depot, and one night the monotony of things, or the activity of the "Red Caps" [military police], made the Aussies and NZs forget how docile they really were, and there was a "lively night on the Bedford front" [not the western front]. A couple of hundred Aussies, NZs and British, chased the Red Caps all round the town and caught some of them at the railway station. Those Red Caps got it hot!

Well, near about this time things out in France were not looking any too rosy for our old pal "Fritz", and I don't know whether I had a feeling that I wanted to be in "at the death", or whether I was fed up with "playing at soldiers", as that's what we were doing at Bedford in my opinion. So one day I asked to be put in a draft for France again, and was told the order was that no 1914 men were to be used overseas again. And that's that. So I had to carry on with the agony of "baby parades". Kids of about 3 or 4 months service used to parade with the older ones for "flag drill" and us older ones had to do things for these babies benefit that we had learnt and forgot and learnt again, before some of the poor little devils had thoughts of leaving school. Can you wonder at us getting fed up? I well remember the day the Armistice was signed. We were sitting on some benches in a hut having a lecture on field telephones. Ye Gods! Field telephones that had been hanging around my darned neck for years it had seemed while I was over the channel! Telephones that I had kicked, swore at, slept on, dreamed about and a thousand other things, and here they are still stuffing them down our "gills" for the benefit of the young ones. Of course I'm willing to admit the youngsters had to learn the same as we learnt in the old days, but why in the —— couldn't they get up a scheme whereby the young 'uns could have come along steadily, on their own, or did they think the "old hands" were learning something, because I can assure you they were not getting much change out of some of the old 'uns. If a kid asked me direct to sort anything out for him, I would do it with pleasure, but I was too fed up and sick at the sight of helios and lamps, telescopes and "bingos", flags and flappers, and field telephones to go out of my way to show 'em, and the majority of the older ones were too far concerned as to where the "entrance fee" to the pub was coming from to worry much about learning kids signalling.

Armistice November 11th 1918

Well the day Armistice was signed we were at one of those everlasting lectures [or sermons], when the news came over from the HQ that Fritz had "done the needful" and had "signed articles". It was about 11.30am as roughly as I can guess now, when we had the news from an officer entering the hut and saying that the Germans had signed. We gave a "whoop" and were told we could break away and come to the parade after dinner as usual at 2.00pm. Now reader I ask you. We used to finish parades at 12.00 for the morning, it was now about 11.30 and we were being given half an hour's holiday to celebrate the Armistice. The youngsters who had not been over the channel were of course delighted to think they were knocking off half an hour earlier than usual, and ran out kicking their heels up like a lot of lambs looking for mamma. But I remember there were dozens of old hands there that had been out there some long time, and some from the start as I had. Was it fair or just, was it human, to expect these men to be satisfied with half an hour's holiday to celebrate all we had been through during those war years in France? Of course it wasn't, and the old hands, myself included, adjourned to the nearest pub. [Oh yes, I can drink a pint as well as anyone else when there is a vital question to be settled, such as this was, although I have got medals for belonging [once], to the Army Temperance Association.] Reader, I hear you say "you old hypocrite"? So over a "pint of poison" in which some of the boys in khaki found relief, we decided that as far as we were concerned that the 12 noon parade and all those connected with it could go to a place "mentioned in despatches" [but not officially]. I've heard it's warm there too! That proposal was carried and duly stamped with "ave another one", and, of course, by the time "chucking out" came we were all merry and bright and didn't care for old "Von Kluck". We made our way to our billets in a more or less orderly way, as we were all billeted in empty houses in different streets just the same as the other "respectable citizens" 'hic, of Bedford was, "sho there", and got our utensils, knife, fork, spoon, pick, shovel, etc and went to the hut for dinner. One or two "little affairs" occurred at dinner that called for the attentions of the regimental police, but beyond a few black eyes and many swear words, and a bit of broken crockery where someone "ever so gently" upset a table loaded with plates, there was "nothing to report". So after the "lions" had fed up we sloped off again back to our billets and from there, those of us who had decided not to go on parade went to Bedford Park out of the way till the parade had fell in and marched off. That was that, so far. At night, of course, we had another right royal time with the aid of a few thousand other troops and civvies. And next morning, of course, we paraded as usual with the rest of the squads in Bushmead Avenue, Bedford, ready to take our gruel, as of course we knew we had something to come.

All the rest of the squads were marched off to their respective drill grounds and this left only our little bunch standing all forlorn in the street. I can see the scene now as tho' it was only this morning. There was our little squad, about 30 strong, of which half had gone on yesterday's 2.00 pm parade [as we had led the young ones astray], and half had not. And there was the Colonel surrounded by his disciples composed of a couple of spare Captains, the Adjutant, and a few spare 2nd Lieutenants, of which rank there were plenty roaming harmlessly about Bedford doing nothing but draw the pay [I nearly said dole]; although it was to a certain extent "dole" as they were getting it for doing nothing. Well there we were all ready for receiving the "goods", and the Colonel and the rest trying to decide what sort of "goods" to deliver. Presently he came and stood in front of the squad and spake unto us these words. "So this is the squad that decided to celebrate the Armistice in their own particular manner is it"? He said it in that sarcastic way that made me long to blurt out "Yes you big bladder, and we did". But I didn't say it. Somebody in one of the rear ranks made a noise like a ram bleating, but the old man let it pass, altho' he must have heard it. Somebody else giggled presumably at the thoughts of the day before. The "old man" then said he hoped we had enjoyed ourselves [the liar], and that he hoped we would further enjoy ourselves by doing guard that same night after parade, and on Saturday afternoon we could do the parade we didn't do yesterday. With that he said, "March off" and turned away quick to hide a grin over his ugly chivvy. I suppose he thought he had done something big in front of some of those smooth baby faced 2nd Lt's that were hovering around. We were marched off by our Sergeant to the parade ground whistling "Tipperary" and "Pack up your troubles" and as we caught up with the Colonel in the street and the Sergeant said "Eyes left" we still kept on singing "Pack up your troubles". He didn't halt us, but he called the Sergeant to him and said something. We thought he might have said "Forgive them for me Sergeant, and give them a kiss all round", but it wasn't it, and we had to do that guard and parade. Now we used to mount guard at Bedford each night at 5pm, so we were on parade that afternoon until 4pm then we had to walk nearly a mile from the parade ground to our different billets, dash across to the dining hall to get our dear teas, rush to the stores and get rifle ammunition and bandoliers, dash back to the billet to give it a "rub over", roll our blankets and greatcoat and mount guard at 5pm. Reader just try doing that lot for once, in an hour, and see if you can turn out "spotless" like the pigheaded Sergeant-Major of B Company. RE Signals, Bedford, expected us to turn

out that November night. He choked us all off as the dirtiest lot he'd ever
seen [the one eyed kaffir], altho' we tried to explain things; he simply said,
"That did not concern him". Reader he made me so mad that I said to the
chum next to me in a "stage whisper", "I'd like to meet him in civil life
soon", and he overheard it. Not that I cared a hang then. To show me he
heard it, he said, "Perhaps you'll get your chance some day lad". I said, "I
hope so to", and I do. They tell me he has silver plate in his head. If I meet
him he might want a silver plate all over. The reason I write in such a
"cheerful" way towards that Company Sgt Major is this. We all done that
guard as a punishment, so we were not squirming over taking our
medicine, but at the way in which that heathen "bullied us" for not being
spick and span as we should have been at an ordinary time. To make me
feel a bit more "nice" towards him, he and I met the very next day on the
road leading to the dining hut, and on my left arm I wore three strips of
khaki braid denoting that I had done 12 years service with good conduct
[three GC badges. Swank], and spotting this he said "we want a few of the
old school in this place to liven things up a bit", and yet he had treated the
boys of the "old school" like schoolboys the day before. I've seen better
men than him drawing "rickshaws" about the streets of Tientsin and
Pekin. And to help matters to accumulate a little more I was detailed for
my ordinary guard after the Saturday afternoon parade. [I did enjoy
celebrating the Armistice, didn't I?]

Well this is Armistice week 1918 and I was daily getting more fed up with
playing at soldiers so I put in for a course of fast reading which would get
those who passed a "staff job" as cycle orderly to the quarter master. He
was more human than all the rest of them at Bedford put together. I had a
big kitchen in an empty house all to myself, and used the kitchen range for
my own convenience. I lived and slept in that house in the Goldington
Road, Bedford, for nearly three months, which got me around to
February 1919 when I was demobbed. But I'm going ahead just a little too
fast.

When I first went to Bedford we were put in a camp opposite the Depot
of the Bedford out Kempston way[35], and there never was an over flush of
food knocking around at that time [probably owing to the fact that the
Brass Hats knew that Fritz was on the point of chucking in the sponge, and
that being the case the troops would not be needed to fatten up for
killing]. Anyway, after every meal we could be seen dashing down the

Kempston Road to a little shop for some tea and a big bread and butter roll which a "motherly old soul" used to sell for 3d. She was besieged every day, and nearly all day by different parties of troops between parades all clamouring for "grub". I should not think the coming generation of Bedford would be in a hurry to join up if the present day ones tell them about it all. Maybe you are thinking I am a bit of a "wolf", but I was one of hundreds who used to take part in the stampede to the "grub shop". Why the Christmas dinner I had in a dugout not a mile from Fritz was a better affair than the one we had in Bedford in 1918. The old lady at Kempston had a shop full of troops that day.

Well now, I carried on as QM's orderly until one day in February 1919 an orderly from HQ came to the billet and told me I was for demobilisation at 10am next day, and, honestly speaking, I was sorry to hear it. So after the necessary signing of "death warrants" and getting a bundle of papers stuffed in my hand and being medically examined, I was packed off with a few more to the big demobilisation camp at Fovand, being finally discharged from the Army after 12 years and 4 months of the most interesting time of my life, "a serving of His Majesty the King". For my share of the war, reader, I had £31-10/- of which £26-10/- was my gratuity and £5 deffered pay. After all now, come to think of it, I fancy I earned it too. I have often wondered what the Canadians, Australians, New Zealanders and South Africans got in money when they settled up, and if that yarn was true about each of them receiving £500 gratuity. If they did, jolly good luck to them. But I know Tommy Atkins did not.

CHAPTER 18

A "Brave New World"

Well, on my return to civilian life, and after a month's leave, I started at my old job again. The returned ones who joined up before a certain date in 1914 had the useful little sum of £10 given them, BUT only if they were single men. If you were unfortunately married and joined up at once, on the bugle sounding as it were, you were then unlucky as regards the 10 "Fishers" or "Bradburys" as the case may be. It's only fair to mention that the wives of the married men had been drawing a small sum per week, perhaps, and therefore I suppose it was too much for the "poor old married men" to expect a finger in the £10 pie. That's one handicap of being married. The others I'd better not mention as the "missus" might read this, and although she never had a chance to enter for her 1st class army education certificate, she can read between the lines, like she did when I hadn't got a "green envelope", and the censor was busy.

Well, the old firm gave us a big dinner one night to celebrate the occasion of how we won the war, and so on, thanks very much, and everybody was merry and bright. "Community singing" with the "very pathetic" song, "for he's a jolly good fellow" being sung by all every 5 minutes, and then, of course the novelty wears off everything in time, and you go back to work to find what? To find men in there who don't know the colour of khaki, never heard the boom of a gun, the crack of a bullet, or the scream of a shell or a bomb. Who had never seen their best pals lying dead around them, lying there torn, maimed, gashed, and bleeding. Who had never had the honour of giving a pal his last drink, before he goes across the "Great Divide". Who had never seen through their tears the sight of mothers and daughters struggling across the fields around Mons pushing babies along in "prams" and getting shot down by a bullet and shrapnel the same as we were; mothers maybe who had their husbands and sons away elsewhere in

France doing their bit. To such men as these I can only say "what did you do in the Great War?" One individual had the cheek, or ignorance, to say to a pal of mine these words "There don't seem to have been many of you killed, as there is plenty of you coming back to your jobs". We are all three working in the same department, so I can prove that any time. That from a man who hid, as a lot more of them did, behind the banner of "INDESPENSABLES. That was the remark from an "indespensable" to an "Old Contemptible". I've often wished he had said it to me, instead of having it repeated to me. But I suppose it is the way of the world, so still being a believer in the old motto "Honi soi qui mal y pense", I suppose we must take it for granted. I sometimes think how nice it would be for another "Great War" to come along just for the doubtful pleasure of sitting back and watching others go up and have a fist at it. Or maybe just so I could work all hours of the day and night on munitions and earn my £5 or £6 or even £7 per week and more, and then buy my own house, and several more besides over the heads of other people, and then, when all those "silly fools" who went out to fight for their "King and Country" came home again, how nice it would be to let them have these houses at my price of letting. Either that or let them go and live in rooms like any other man and his wife and 3 or 4 kiddies has to if he was "fool enough to fight". I wonder. Would I enjoy myself? Are these the people enjoying themselves who did all the things that I have just described? I don't think they can be, for I see them walking about daily with looks on their faces such as you would see on the face of a peddler who had just sold his last box 'o lights for a 1d and then spots the old gent coming up the road who always gives him a "tanner" for a box. If you speak to 'em they tell you they have never seen such rotten times as these, they say such things as, they want new boots, they want new clothes, their kids want this, they want that, and yet I have been told these very men were earning, or at least getting, anything from £7 to £10 per week during the war making munitions, and we lads were getting our modest 1/- per diem all found, even to the mud. Maybe it's coming home to some of the "conscientious objectors" at last. I think the great secret of it is this; they have never travelled, and travel is a fast teacher. They have never had to fend for themselves. They have always gone along in the same old rut day after day, get up, go to work, come home, and go to bed. Tomorrow repeat the dose. Maybe it's that which has deadened their minds and their brains to the extent of helping others, but not to the extent of helping themselves. They grow self centred and egoistic. Either that, or they are nothing but a heap of lying, cringing, hypocrites. I'm "chugging along" on a merry old tin full of money each week [but it's a very small tin!] and my weekly takings are the magnificent sum of £1-17-3. The rent I pay is 10/- per week and the rates help me out with another 2/9d. Am I moaning? Of course not! I have a wife and three kiddies all at school [the kiddies not the missus!]. The missus does her bit and earns a few bob chucking the soap and flannel about for a few clients, and I get an extra bob or two at pushing worms back into their holes on a couple of gardens for some "gents", and tell them it's gardening. So, I ask you, reader, what is there to grouse about? My kiddies want this, and my kiddies want that, I want this and that, and the missus wants this and that, but we don't get it, so what we never have we never miss. I'm never really "broke" as I have a farthing I dug up in a garden once, but I'm often badly "bent" after Tuesday. Still there are two sides to every question, just the same as there is to flypaper [as the fly said before he pitched], and if I had a lot of money I should only go and spend it, whereas now I can watch others spend theirs, and get cheated. Mr Henry Ford, of Detroit USA, has, so I've heard, quite a lot of money. Yet I read in the paper that another motor car has crashed into Mr Ford's car, as he was driving home one day, and knocked him over a bank with a twenty foot drop, and I've got the consolation of knowing that such a thing could never possibly happen to me as I should not be in a motor car driving home from work. I always use "Shank's pony". So money does not save you from getting knocked about. [Ask Jack Dempsey if he does.]

CHAPTER 19

Reprise

Now reader, be you lady or gentleman, I have written this diary from an "Old Contemptibles" point of view, and with just the ordinary British Tommy's pre-war standard of education. I was not born with a silver spoon in my mouth, neither was I born with a pencil and pen in each hand, so if I have put in too much impolite language to suit some people, I can only say I have been much more polite in my choice of language than the people who uttered it were, so let's leave it at that. Maybe if I am lucky enough to get this in print I shall have a few old pals chasing after me as critics when they find out who I am, and maybe again I shall not.

I do not care who reads it, as all names can be had from me for the asking. I would on my honour willingly go through it again, providing I knew I should finish up as I did [all in one lump!]. I have an idea that joining the service is the one and only way for a young lad, of poor circumstances, to see the world for free and all found. What more could a young lad of 19 or 20 years of age, as I was then, desire than to be "dumped" down on the pretty island of Malta on a glorious November day, with the knowledge that he was going to spend three years there "exploring" the island. What more do you need than to see the sweating "coolies" at Port Said "coaling" ships while you lean on the rails and laugh at them, and on again through the canal to Suez town. What prettier sight could you wish for than to see a string of liners and cargo boats going down the Suez Canal at night, each with a big searchlight fixed at the bows, or to be in the same canal by day to see the sights of the Bitter Lakes, and the different tribes that live along the canal?

What more can you want than to go through the Red Sea where it makes you gasp for breath, being just a little hotter than Heligoland [without the 'igoland attached!], to see a school of "sea pigs" [porpoises] leaping and dashing round the old boat as she ploughs her way along? Or to see a shark fight in the Gulf of Aden, or to go ashore at Columbo in Ceylon and see the little black naked kiddies running about there? Or to see the natives diving from up on the boat deck into the harbour, amongst the jelly-fish, for silver coins? Or to feel the old boat heaving and rolling under you as she steps out into what "Jack" calls a "snorter" on the way across to Penang, and on down through the Straits to Singapore, and then to gaze at the little studded islands with coconut trees growing down to the waters edge? Away we go again up to Hong Kong and what more could you want than to go for a walk up around the wooded hills of the Peak? Or to see the race-course, and to swipe at butterflies in all colours of the rainbow as large as your own two hands? Or to see your pal pitched out of a rickshaw on his nose for taking liberties with his coolie runner? All these things I have seen, reader, free gratis and for nixes.

Aboard we go again, and the old "tub" steps it out once more up the Yellow Sea on her way north. Now she feels it, rolling and pitching down into it, and shaking her head, the good old *Somali* comes up again throwing fountains of dirty, yellow ocean off her bows. Reader 'twas glorious. Five or six days of it squirming and twisting her old nose away up north. Pass Port Arthur close in on Sunday evening, and away across the big Gulf, and then at last we come alongside the jetty at Chingwangtao. Hullo China! Here we are then, and now we hop on board a train and have a run up the line to Tientsin. Tientsin is reached and smell the garlic! Now gaze at the mob of grinning "chinks" and see if you can tell the 'tother from which. Watch them dance about like big babies at a school treat. Your "John Chinaman", reader, is a big baby at heart, and as faithful a servant as you can find [if you treat him properly]. Go for a ride in a rickshaw sitting behind a coolie on a warm day, him stripped to the waist, and see the sweat pour from his gleaming brown body. Tell him to take you to the French Arsenal somewhere about 5 or 6 miles out from Tientsin, and tell him to "Dong a Dong" [wait for you] until you have seen all the days sports, and then run you back home again. Give him one "big" dollar, one to ten at that time, and see the "delight" shining through the slits holding his eyes. Would you do that reader for a "Chink"?

Take a hand at breaking in a few Mongolian ponies straight down from the hills of Mongolia; never heard a white man's voice before, maybe, and mad with terror some of them at the sound of it.

Get on one of 'em's back after breaking it in, and then go on a three day patrol hunting up missionaries and such like while the revolution[36] was on in 1911 and 1912. Get away up on the international ranges at Pekin for a fortnight having a shoot for the Empire Cup.

Go for a months manoeuvres in the Gobi Desert, North China, and sleep in the sand there and feel the monkey nuts poking into your ribs, scratch away the sand, pick 'em and eat 'em, they are yours.

Reader, that's the life for you, much better than lining up for the "dole". Have a day's outing and go for a donkey ride into Pekin from the ranges. Take the old moke up, away up the long steps leading to the bazaar and buy a few curios, and "pinch" a few more [if you can].

Now let me post you on "sentry go" away up on the "Camel's Bridge" at Fengtai, North China, at the height of the revolution. Let me give you your orders – "stop everyone from coming over this bridge tonight". Now listen carefully during the small hours of the night and you can hear a steady pad, pad, pad of feet coming towards you in the darkness. "Halt. Who goes there?" you yell. No answer. You slip one round into the breech of your gun, and come down to the "ready". Once more, "Halt. Who goes there?" No answer, and now you're getting the "wind up". You have visions of two-edged swords and you picture your head cut off lying in the snow. Finger on the trigger you come up to the aim, shut your eyes, hope for the best and, yes, when you open your eyes again you see a poor old Chinese beggar woman, ugly as sin, scared to death, falling along in the snow towards you. There are no standing army orders to the effect that you must shoot an old defenceless Chinese beggar woman, but she must not pass. She jabbers away at you, and you answer, "Yes I know all about that", but you don't know a word she says. So call out the guard. "Guard turn out". Results? Chinese prisoner captured by me at midnight on the British front. That little drama actually happened to me one night on "sentry go" in China, and wasn't I proud of my capture.

Now let me take you for an evening stroll when you are off duty, and we go along the platform at Fengtai station just as the "Trans Siberian" train pulls in on the way up to Pekin. Hear a dear little English baby girl say to her mother, "Oh look, Mummy. English soldiers all out here", and you give them a smile and a wave of your hand, and touch your helmet to her parents. Reader I honestly believe now that that little girl's voice was about the first English youngster's voice [other than military] that I had heard for over a year. I shall never forget that pretty little kiddies face as she stood on the veranda at the rear of the railway carriage. That occurred fifteen years ago and it's still fresh in my memory. We had grown so used to seeing nothing but yellow hordes of Chinese faces, day after day, that to see that dear little girl's face surrounded by its pretty curls, was like seeing an angel from heaven, smiling at you as you "booked your passage" to the other place "lower down". That kiddy made me feel good for once.

Now reader, let me invite you to take a hand in a game of cards sitting on the veranda of a bungalow till midnight or till 1, 2, or 3 in the morning. You may ask "Why till that time?" and I'll tell you. Try going to sleep inside your mosquito net inside the bungalow any old night in July or August, or September up in Tientsin. Just try it for a week, and then see if it isn't more preferable to sit out and play cards. When the temperature is somewhere about 2000 [more or less] in the shade see if you can stand the pressure of a handkerchief on your sweating back. The other side of the picture comes about Christmas and just after. Let me take you to the wash-house at the end of the bungalow. Now have a swill in the bowl, and now dash back to your room and see if you can comb your hair without standing in front of the fire to thaw it. See your hair in the mirror all standing stiff and frozen just because you had to run 20 yards in the open air. That's the winter up there.

Let me show you the oxen that draws the water cart with icicles hanging from it's nostrils, and it's hot breath freezing as it falls. Cold weather about now I guess. Let me take you to the frozen lake at the back of the stables and see nearly a battalion of troops playing on the ice without a crack in it, and a wagon weighing a couple of tons empty, but loaded with a couple of tons of stable manure, and 10 or 12 oxen pulling it across the frozen lake without going through the ice. Nice thick ice about now. All these things I've seen reader, for nixes.

Now let me take you for a nights "boozing expedition". Let's go up the Taku Road, Tientsin, and call in at old Rebecca Swartz, the fat German woman, who keeps the "Hotel Bristol", Taku Road, Tientsin. Here we are then; "What's yours?" Two bottles of beer, one dollar gone bang. It's a hot sultry night so we will have a sit down. Lets have another to drown the other one. Now we are comfortable. The door opens. In come two of three Tommies, "Enniskillen Fusiliers", followed by some "Yankee" troops. Later on French, German and other troops come in till the noise resembles an open-air market. Everybody jabbering away at once in their own lingo. Now things are just starting to hum with a capital H. Beer is running swiftly but smoothly in the required direction, and eyes are beginning to shine. One "English nightingale" starts a song, then another, and so on round the long bar. A "Froggie" wants to sing, but because the pig-headed English troops cannot understand him, he doesn't get on very well with it. Then "Fritz" tries his hand and he gets the "bird". Words are followed by fists, fists are followed by boots and belts, which in turn leads to flying bottles and glasses, and tables going over. A "Fritz" gets flung head over heels behind the piano, Rebecca screams, the "Red Caps" rush in and clear us all out and poor old Rebecca Swartz, the fat German lady, finds her pub "out of bounds" for a month or so. What do you want more than that reader? If you are not satisfied read on.

Now let me take you in another direction. Imagine yourself my pal for a couple of hours and we are in the Infantry Barracks, Tientsin, and it's the afternoon of Christmas Day 1911. This is how yourself and me would have a beano. My pal and I were bored stiff with nothing to do after we had eaten our heads off at dinner time, so although we were not what you call regular "canteen Wallas", that is regular boozers [although we did not mind "bathing our lips" at intervals], we suddenly decided to clean up and go out. Suiting the action to the word we left the Barracks and jumped into a rickshaw each and told the coolies to run us down to the French concession for a little bit of business we had to attend to, something like seeing a lady about a dog, only more so. We particularly impressed upon the coolies that we did not want to go to the Japanese concession, as that place was posted in orders as out of bounds to British troops. Of course, "Wun Lung" or "Sai When" or whatsoever the coolies name was "Ya me savvy, plenty flesh, plenty flesh". Also we thought he was saying, "He savvied, plenty French, plenty French". So away we goes all merry and bright by the long roundabout way eventually arriving at the darned Jap concession that was "out of bounds". I thought some of the house looked familiar, and I yelled to my pal [who lives in Bath by the way], "Hi kid I believe the darned chinks have brought us by a strange route to the Jap "concess." He was thinking the same himself, and we were trying to decide whether to swing round and go back, or go on and chance our arm, when two military policemen strolled the corner about 50 yards ahead of us. That decided us all right. My pal was in a rickshaw in front and promptly he yelled to his coolie "Bights you ———. Turn around and run quick". His coolie evidently tumbled to the situation, which was lucky for us, and turning round quick he nearly bowled my coolie, rickshaw and all, over into the mud. Away we all fled back the route we came and the British residents of Tientsin around the British quarters were treated to the sight of two coolies and rickshaws [all part worn], and two British Tommies [one an NCO, not me], also part worn, speeding away from the Japanese concession at about 40 knots an hour, more or less, right away up to the "Soldier's Home", where we went in for tea. I may add that we did pay those coolies, but not with money. Now reader here's a penny for you to go across to the cookhouse and get me five fried eggs for tea. That's all the money you need, so you'll get 'em alright for that, 5 cents to a penny, eggs 1 cent each, or would you prefer a chicken, or maybe a duck, if so here's 20 cents [4d] to go and buy one cooked in the "all in" fashion, viz, only "plucked" and leave the rest to you.

Maybe reader by now you are feeling homesick, so let's leave the land of mystery [China] and come across the sea with me to Malta, the land of goats. We, you and I, and a few hundred other "worlds policemen" arrive off Malta on the 12th of November 1908. We pull into the harbour and anchor in the Sliema Creek. We have not been in the island long before we get a shock. The Messina earthquake 1908. Another fine sight we have is the burning off the harbour mouth of the *SS Sardinia*, a Pilgrim ship. We see all the bodies being tugged up through the harbour several days later. Let's take a trip to visit the "Chapel of Bones", and see all the "grinning skulls" and a couple of skeletons standing up in the corner. What prettier crowd could you wish for than to see the crowd at the Army and Navy "soccer" match in Malta. The Tommies in red tunics and "white toppees", and Jack in his blue, blended with all the different colours of the Maltese population. Have a trip on the Valetta to Imtarfa express [4d all the way] in and out of people's gardens knocking the washing off the clothesline [or nearly so]. Malta, reader, is a glorious little spot. A pal of mine "liked" Malta so much that he wrote some poetry about it, something like this.

Malta the land of cursed drink

Three glasses book you for the "clink" [guard room]
Land of robbers, without a doubt
I've cursed the place since I've been out
Land of people with bare, big feet
Land where soldiers drill in cruel heat
Land of filth and goats galore
Serving our fever more and more

He must have liked the place evidently!

Well now reader, I've said before in this narrative that all things good and bad must come to an end, so I am hoping for the sake of anyone who has the courage and inclination to read this diary from the beginning that they will be rewarded well for doing so in the knowledge that it is written all in good faith and without fear of favour to anyone concerned.

So we will make just one more little call on our way home to England and step ashore at Gibraltar for a few hours. All I saw of Gib was up through the Whale Bone Arch, passing the Governor's House somewhere on the left, into a pub with more pals, and I was told we could not be served as it was after hours. So we had a "Gharry" ride to the "Ramps", and there found solace, after which time flew so quick that the boat nearly left us behind. So that's the Rock of Gibraltar for me. Now we are back aboard and in about a day and a half hope to be ploughing thro' the Bay. Now we're thro', coming up channel, see the lights of old England to greet us after our stay out East. Southampton at last.

Hurrah for "civvy life". But is it Hurrah? I don't think so, not now I've had some. Not now I've had to mix with those of a cramped outlook. Those who do not know the meaning of "muck in", or 50-50. Those who are all for themselves and damn the one behind. Those who creep and crawl up to the foreman and the manager's leg to keep their noses from being pushed out of joint. I often wonder to myself what sort of life some of these men would have lived out there during the four years of killing? Would they have shared their fags and parcels as we did, would they have shared their last franc as with a pal as we did? Judging by the appearance of their grasping, grabbing now, I can only say "they would not". Give me the real servicemen for pals and I'd be content, but no man coming from the service today is going to be content with his life amongst robbing, greedy conscientious objectors who[37] he has to work with or starve. I have asked several ex-servicemen of both services, and they are of the same mind towards them. In fact, if some of the remarks were put down here, the book would not stand the strain. The majority of these "stay at home don't fight" seem to look upon the average ex-service man as an interloper who has no right looking for work, but should have been killed off and out of the way; so we did not get ourselves killed just to spite them. So reader as you will doubtless remember, I set out to see the world. I've not seen it all I admit, but what I've seen cost me nothing, and I'm feeling just as fit and eager today as I felt when I was a kid of 18. So hoping that all you youngsters who read this will get away and have a peep at the "Globe".

I bid you "adieu" from

   An "Old Contemptible."

Notes

1   Plug Street was the Diggers [Australians] name for Ploegsteert in Belgium near Ypres.

2   The Old Contemptibles
The name adopted by British troops belonging to the regular army in 1914 and supposedly derived from a comment made by the German Kaiser, Wilhelm II. The Kaiser, upon hearing that German forces were being held up, is said to have exclaimed his exasperation of "Sir John French's contemptible little army". This term was probably due to a combination of exasperation and anxiety he felt about how well the Schlieffen Plan was being implemented, and that it was being held up by the resistance of the much smaller British Army. By the end of 1914 the BEF had almost ceased to exist with 90% casualties and 30% dead.

3   *SS Rohilla*
The *Rohilla* had been a passenger ship working the route between London and Calcutta, but in August 1914 *Rohilla* was requisitioned and converted for use as a Hospital Ship. On the 29th of October she left Leith bound for Dunkirk to board wounded but at 0400 the following day she ran aground on the Saltwick Nab, near Whitby. Although this was attributed to a German mine this was propaganda, as, in reality, the *Rohilla* had lost it's way due to the absence of coastal lights, ran onto a sand bank and broke it's back.

4   On 28 December 1908 an earthquake, quickly followed by a tsunami, almost completely destroyed the cities of Messina, on the eastern coast of Sicily, and Reggio on the Italian mainland looking across the Messina Straits. Very many of these fatalities occurred in Messina where about one third of its 150,000 inhabitants died.

5   H.O JONES was a crew member rescued from the *S.S. Sardinia* disaster. The ship sailed out of Grand Harbour at about 10 a.m on Wednesday November 25th 1908 with 39 crew, 12 saloon passengers, and 142 Moroccans travelling to Mecca. About 200 yards out she caught fire and was hit by a number of explosions, and then she ran aground and suffered a huge explosion. Since it was too dangerous for rescue boats to go alongside, passengers and crew had to jump into the sea into the sea. 10

passengers and 23 crew were saved, but over 100 Moroccan Arabs died.

6   Somerset Light Infantry [Prince Albert's Light Infantry]
        During the Great War this Regiment formed no less than 19 Battalions. Many
        fought in Europe, but some were sent to India and the Middle East. The Regiment
        had nearly 5000 casualties in the 1st World War.

        They had their celebration ditty!
        "We are the boys of Old Somerset
        We've stuck it ten months and we're sticking it yet.
        Our founder Prince Albert, a King but in name,
        But the good old swede bashers still add to their fame.
        I hope you don't think we're chucking a hint,
        But I think you'll admit we are hard as flint.
        They call us the Sets but we don't care a fig,
        As long as they find us some trenches to dig.
        PA's on our cab badge and don't think we're barmy
        When we say that the meaning is Pride of the Army"

        The Somerset's were also known as the "Light Bobs", or the old "Stonewallers".

7   Solesmes is a town in the Nord Department. The 2nd South Lancs and the 1st Wilts
        were attacked at Solesmes on the evening of the 24th August 1914.

8   Mons
        In August 1914 the 70,000 strong BEF met the advancing German Army at Mons,
        near Charleroi in Belgium. The British Commander Sir John French deployed the
        BEF east and west of Mons on a 40km front. To stop the advancing Germans, orders
        were given to destroy the bridges over the Mons-Condé Canal. The British troops
        were roughly dug in along the canal and amongst the mining villages and slagheaps
        and on August 23rd the German attack began, with artillery barrages followed by
        massed infantry attacks. The BEF defended magnificently, cutting down the dense
        ranks of oncoming Germans with sustained rifle fire and they gained little ground.
        The strength and rapidity of British rifle fire was such that the Germans believed
        they were being fired on with machine guns (of which there were, in fact, only two
        per battalion) and many German regiments were utterly decimated by the end of
        the battle. The British force of 70,000 men and 300 guns had been outnumbered by
        some 150,000 German troops and 600 guns. There had been some 1,600 casualties
        on the British side and between 5000 and 10,000 Germans became casualties.
        Nevertheless, by the evening it had become apparent to French that the BEF was
        facing an enemy far superior in numbers, and that if contact with the French was
        not to be completely lost, a retreat would have to be ordered.

        Another, larger-scale, battle took place at Le Cateau on 26 August, where British
        casualties reached were about 8000. Although the BEF once again inflicted
        extremely heavy losses on von Kluck's army, there was no option but to continue

the retreat all the way back toward Paris. From this point until 5 September, the hungry, exhausted BEF was constantly on the move, often forced to fight its pursuers as it retreated over 200 miles of the Belgian and French countryside, a retreat graphically recorded in these diaries. In the 2nd WW Churchill said about Dunkirk that you don't win wars by evacuation and retreat, but the Retreat from Mons allowed the BEF to remain in France, and probably saved the vital Channel ports. The BEF retreated to the River Marne.

9   Charles Bertie Prowse
Charles Bertie Prowse joined the 2nd Battalion Somerset Light Infantry and served in the South African War. By August 1914 he had reached the rank of major and was serving with the 1st battalion of his regiment, with which he went to war as part of 11th Brigade, 4th Division. He took part in the early battles of the war and lent his name to a farm – Prowse Point – at Ploegstreet Wood, near Ypres, and the only cemetery in the Ypres Salient to be named after a person is Prowse Point Military Cemetery. Briefly he commanded 1st Battalion Leinster Regiment, but in April 1915 he returned to 4th Division as GOC 11th Brigade. He had risen from junior major to Brigadier-General in 9 months. Like many other formations in VIII Corps, 11th Brigade met with disaster on 1 July1916 on the Somme. Brigadier-General Prowse was mortally wounded by a German machine gun firing from the Ridge Redoubt, north of Beaumont Hamel, after moving his brigade HQs into the former German front line trench, believing it clear of the enemy. All the brigade's battalion commanders were also killed or wounded in the attack. Prowse's brother, Captain Cyril Prowse RN, had also been killed a month earlier in the explosion of his ship, *HMS Queen Mary*, at the Battle of Jutland.

10   Le Cateau
The Battle of Le Cateau was essentially a rearguard action fought by the British in late August 1914, during the general Allied retreat. General Smith-Dorrien decided to stand and fight the German 1st Army under Von Kluck. The BEF had been in fighting retreat for several days and was very fatigued. Smith-Dorrien's decision was against the orders of Sir John French to continue the retreat. The battle began on August 26th, and the British sustained 7,812 casualties, losses were high on the German side as well, and the action further delayed the planned German advance on Paris, and the British were able to disengage in some order. The British tactic of rifle fire from shallow trenches is well described in the diaries, and had been a feature of the Battle of Mons as well. This battle was part of the background to the Battle of the Marne soon after, a battle that led to the creation of the Western Front. The Germans had been stopped but not beaten, and any hopes for a swift end to the war were shattered.

11   St Quentin
On August 1, 1914 the announcement of general mobilization surprised the population of the Saint-Quentin region. The presence of the 87th infantry regiment since 1876 and the proximity of the Artillery at La Fère made the people feel safe, but at the end of August 1914, however, the region was occupied and the Germans

set up defence lines. Between offensives and counter-offensives, the region was cut in half by the Hindenburg line and was ruined. This region was cleared of the enemy in October 1918.

12   Bucy-le-Long was in the department of Aisne close to Soissons.

13   Jack Johnson's were German artillery guns that used shells that produced a massive black cloud when exploding; Jack Johnson was a famous large black American boxing champion with a legendary powerful punch.

14   Caverne du Dragon: An old quarry that was used as an underground barracks by the Germans with sniper positions, hospital, dormitories, etc.

15   Zouaves were French Colonial troops noted for their colourful uniforms, but this swashbuckling bravado died a death in the early months of the war when some Zouave Battalions lost as many as 800 men in a single charge, with bravery being little match against artillery and machine guns. In 1915 the red kepi gave way to a steel helmet, and the blue and red uniforms were replaced by horizon blue. Camouflage not colour became the main criteria.

16   St. Omer is a large town 45 kilometres south-east of Calais.

17   Cassel
In the First World War, General Haig used Cassel as his headquarters during the key battles of Flanders that stemmed the German advance and stopped them occupying this part of France and the neighbouring corner of Belgium.

18   Nieppe is a village close to Armentières. The bridge at Pont-de-Nieppe was seized by the Hampshires on 16 October 1914 and the village then stayed within the Allied lines until 11 April 1918, when the Germans won it back in the Spring Offensive. Nieppe was recaptured by the British on 3 September 1918.

19   Coal box; in army parlance this referred to the 15cm heavy howitzer shells used by the German Army in WW1.

20   "A better 'ole!"
By Bruce Bairnsfather, this is possibly the best-known cartoon of the War. It was certainly known by the hero of these diaries.

21   Ypres was a small Belgium market town that had seen more glorious days, but it became the location of some of the worst fighting of the war, and it is estimated that 500,000 died in a 25 square kilometre salient. Its importance lay in its proximity to the Channel ports and shipping lanes and Britain could not afford to lose control of these. It also became a symbol of Belgium resistance to Germany being the last part of their country still controlled by them.

"Well, if you knows of a better 'ole, go to it."

"A better 'ole!"

The Ypres area at the time was often described as being like a saucer, with the town of Ypres at centre where the cup sits and the surrounding land being the saucer rim. This gives a very good indication of the advantages the Germans had for the greater part of the conflict in this area.

Although fighting in the Ypres sector was continuous throughout, historians have divided the conflict up into battles. These being:

First Battle of Ypres (1914)
Second Battle of Ypres (1915)
Third Battle of Ypres or sometimes known as Passendale (1917)
Fourth Battle of Ypres as part of the German Spring Offensive (1918)
The Final Breakout (1918)

In Zillebeke Church near Ypres there is the following appropriate adage. "Life is a city of crooked streets, death is the market place where all men meet".

22   Doullens is a town about 30 kilometres north of Amiens, in the Somme. Doullens was Marshal Foch's headquarters early in the First World War and where a

conference in March 1918 led to Foch being in charge of all Allied armies on the Western Front. From the summer of 1915 to March 1916, Doullens was a junction between the French Tenth Army on the Arras front and the Commonwealth Third Army on the Somme. It was an important railhead.

23   Albert. During WW1 Albert became a British garrison town, and it was from there that the doomed Somme Offensive was launched on July 1st 1916. The town was retaken by the Germans in the Ludendorff Offensive of March 1918, though retaken by the British soon after. Many civilians lived and sheltered in the underground tunnels.

24   Fonquevilliers. "Funky Villas" as the British soldiers knew it was a village on the Somme and extensively used by the British for hospitalisation.

25   Serre. This was another of the nine fortified villages which were part of the objective to be reached and taken on July 1st 1916. Serre was a significant target on that day because from their trenches in front of the village, the Germans had a high view over a wide part of no-man's land, including the part, which would be crossed slightly to the south, in the attack on Beaumont-Hamel and Hawthorne Ridge.

26   "Y" Ravine. This runs east and west about 800 metres south of the village of Beaumont-Hamel, from "Station Road" to the front line of July 1916. It was a deep ravine with steep sides lined with dugouts, and extending two short arms at the west end. The village of Beaumont-Hamel was attacked and reached on the 1st July 1916, by units of the 29th Division [which included the Royal Newfoundland Regiment], but at enormous cost and it could not be held. Today it is part of Newfoundland Park, an area in the care of the Canadian Government.

27   Thiepval is the largest and one of the most emotive memorials for the missing from the Somme Offensive 1916-17. Opened on 31 July 1932 by the Prince of Wales, the Thiepval memorial was and remains the largest British war memorial in the world. The memorial contains the names of 73,357 British and South African men who have no known grave and who fell on the Somme between July 1916 and 20 March 1918. 150ft high and dominating the surrounding area, the memorial was designed by Sir Edward Lutyens.

28   Shell shock. "Shell shock" was a term used by army doctors to describe the mental and physical breakdown that affected at least 80,000 British soldiers in the trenches during the Great War. The symptoms ranged in severity from headaches, tiredness and an inability to concentrate, to complete mental breakdowns. The only "cure" was to rest and recuperate away from the Western Front and the strain of living in trenches, under regular enemy shellfire. Officers were more likely to be treated sympathetically than private soldiers. Many private soldiers were accused of being "cowards" or "malingerers", and some went on to refuse to obey orders (and were punished by court martial), or even commit suicide in despair at their situation.

29   Bray-sur-Somme is a village 9 kilometres southeast of Albert. Bray-sur-Somme fell into German hands in March 1918, but it was retaken by the 40th Australian Battalion on the 24th August.

30   Arras. An important city close to the Somme. It was the scene of much fighting between the Germans and French in 1914, and although the French lost Lens, they retained Arras.

The second battle Arras was in April and May 1917. It was one of the most important campaigns in which the British Army was engaged, yet has been rather overlooked in comparison to the Somme and Flanders. The British Army launched a large-scale attack at Arras as part of a master plan by new French Commander in Chief Robert Nivelle. Although initially successful, it soon got bogged down and became a terribly costly affair. The British attack was against the formidable Hindenburg Line, to which the enemy had recently made a strategic withdrawal. The battle for Vimy Ridge can be counted as part of this campaign in 1917.

31   St Pol-sur-Ternoise. This small town is in the Pas-de-Calais and was a military administrative centre during the whole of the First World War and was taken over by Commonwealth troops from the French in March 1916.

32   Tommy Tickler's jam. This came in 13.2-ounce tins to be shared out by sections. Contrary to the much repeated "the only jam was Tickler's Plum and Apple", a variety of 13.2-ounce tins of jam were available, which included marmalade and assorted berry flavours which, alas, all seemed to taste more of "sugar and colour" than of any fruit. The squat tins were saved and put to a myriad of uses, from trench art, over cups to more tactical uses, such as alarm systems in the wire and the manufacture of jam-tin bombs.

33   March Offensive 1918. After the signing of the Brest-Litovsk Treaty with Russia, Germany was able to withdraw its troops from the Eastern Front. It was decided to use these troops to support a massive offensive on the Western Front. The Central Powers hoped that the 1918 Spring Offensive would enable them to end the war before the United States Army became firmly established in France.

It was decided to attack Allied forces at three points along the front-line: Arras, Lys and Aisne. British soldiers became disillusioned when all the land captured during the offensive at Passchendaele was lost in this German attack. At first the German Army had considerable success and came close to making a decisive breakthrough. However, Allied forces managed to halt the German advance at the Marne in June 1918. After suffering 168,000 casualties during the battle, the exhausted German soldiers were forced to retreat. It was the precursor to what was called the "Black Day in the German Army" in August 1918, and the hastening of the end of the war.

34   Mons Medal. This is the least common medal of the war, and one that was highly coveted, and it is popularly but erroneously known as the Mons Star.

This medal was awarded to all officers, warrant officers, non-commissioned officers and all men of the British and Indian Forces, including civilian medical practitioners, nursing sisters, nurses and others employed with military hospitals; as well as men of the Royal Navy, Royal Marines, Royal Naval Reserve and Royal Naval Volunteer Reserve, who served with the establishment of their unit in France and Belgium between August 5th 1914, and midnight of November 22/23rd, 1914.

The decoration consists of a lacquered bronze star, the uppermost ray of the star taking the form of the imperial crown. Resting on the face of the star is a pair of crossed swords, and, on them, is a circular oak wreath. A scroll winds around the swords: it is inscribed with the date Aug.–Nov. 1914. The ribbon is red merging into white and then into blue.

A bar inscribed "5 Aug. to 22 Nov. 1914" was given to all those who served under fire. Since the same ribbon is used with the 1914-15 Star, holders of the earlier award were permitted to wear a small silver rosette on their ribbon when the decoration itself is not worn. On the medal index cards this is usually noted as the "Clasp and Roses".

35 Joe Clough.
This footnote is put in for local interest but general also, I hope.

Joe Clough was one of the first West Indian immigrants to this country, arriving in 1906. He became the first black bus and taxi driver in England. Joe enlisted in the Army Service Corps at Kempston barracks in 1915, making him one of the first in the area to do so. He drove a field ambulance for four years in the Ypres area, one of the bloodiest arenas of battle in the entire Great War. During his time in Belgium, he was treated as an equal by his fellow soldiers, and was even the captain of the cricket team. Joe was demobbed in 1919, and started work for the National Omnibus Company in Bedford, and became a very well known and popular citizen in what has become one of the most multi-racial towns in the UK. It is a distinct possibility that he knew George Coward, or I would like to think so!

36 Chinese revolution.
The Chinese revolution came about with the collapse of the Manchu dynasty, a result of increasing internal disorders, pressure from foreign governments, and the weakness of central government. A nationalist revolt from 1911 to 1912 led to a provisional republican constitution being proclaimed and a government established in Peking headed by Yuan Shihai. The Kuomintang were faced with the problems of restoring the authority of central government and meeting the challenges from militaristic factions (led by warlords) and the growing communist movement.

37 Conscientious Objectors.
Conscientious objectors, to whom George Coward had such objections, were those who did not want to fight in the war. They were derisively called "Conscies". In 1916 The Government introduced conscription because of the huge casualty lists

there were by then, but there was a "conscience clause" that meant that some were able to miss military service on grounds of conscientious objection. Some objected to war of any sort, some opposed the war with Germany as not being justified, and some objected on religious grounds, such as Quakers. Some did not fight but contributed to the war effort as munition workers at home or in jobs such as medical orderlies at the front. Some did not want to do anything, and they were often interned during the war. George Coward's objection to them was partly patriotic, partly because they didn't do their bit, and partly because they had jobs that he found difficult to acquire at the end of the war.

38   Ambulance Trains
Ambulance trains evacuated the wounded or sick from casualty clearing stations to stationary or base hospitals or to a port of embarkation from where they were conveyed by ambulance ship to the UK. In the early weeks of the war, a number of ambulance trains were improvised by the French railways and placed at the disposal of the British Army. By April 1915, however, three ambulance trains had been made in Britain and supplied to the BEF at private cost. It was then decided that a number of 'standard' trains should be built by various British railway companies to War Office specifications and altogether thirty were eventually sent to the military forces overseas, mostly in France and Flanders.

The 'standard' ambulance train consisted of sixteen cars, including a pharmacy car, two kitchens, a personnel car and a brake and stores van. It accommodated about 400 lying and sitting cases in addition to the RAMC personnel and the train crew.

Each ward car contained thirty-six beds in tiers of three (the 'home' ambulance train had tiers of two). The middle bed folded back to enable sitting cases to use the lower one, thus ensuring flexibility. Apart from feeding casualties and staff, the kitchens could supply fifty gallons of hot water at any time. The train generated its own electricity for lighting and driving overhead fans and all cars were steam heated.

Temporary or improvised ambulance trains were pressed into service when big battles were being fought and during 1916, they and the regular ambulance trains conveyed no fewer than 744,616 sick and wounded from the front areas to the base, making 1581 journeys to do so. During the same period, 16,918 cases were evacuated by ambulance barge.

Boulogne was the principal port of embarkation for the wounded and on one occasion it took only nineteen minutes to unload 123 casualties from a train; on another, 264 casualties were similarly cleared in fifty-three minutes. The main disembarkation ports in the UK were Dover and Southampton. It was reckoned that at the former, the average time to unload a ship of, say, 200 stretcher and 300 walking cases, and place them on board two trains was only two hours. From February 1915 to February 1919, Dover dealt with 1,260,506 casualties, unloaded 4076 boats and loaded 7781 ambulance trains. No fewer than 1,234,248 casualties were handled at Southampton from 24 August 1914 to 31 December 1918 during which period 7822 ambulance trains were despatched. The patients were then sent by one of the twenty 'home standard' ambulance trains, or by an emergency ambulance train, to a 'receiving station' – there were 196 of them – where they were transferred to road vehicles, usually by volunteer first aiders, which took them to their destination hospital.

39   Smoking and the War
Having worked on two sets of diaries about the 1st World War, it becomes clear that whether an officer or from the ranks there were 3 real common factors. Firstly there was the fear of death, or worse in a way, maiming. Second was the squalor of the conditions troops had to fight and live in, and lastly was boredom. Boredom was the result of the fact that war rarely happened along all sectors of the Western Front at the same time, and because time had to be filled in there were repetitive drills and fatigues, such as filling sand bags and trench digging. When they were actually in the front line trenches there was a lot of standing around waiting for something to happen – be they officers or men.

Smoking had been prevalent amongst armies since the 17th century and the authorities saw the morale boost of ensuring that the supply of cigarettes reached the men serving at the front, either from the canteen or from home. Many who had never smoked before the war took up the habit during, and the majority smoked.

The most popular cigarette was the Woodbine, though plenty rolled their own using Rizla cigarette papers.

Undoubtedly tobacco became a "comfort" in a very harsh world, and there was little discussion about the health consequences of this. Also, cigarettes were shared round and became a means of the development of friendships and morale.

Soldiers more and more cupped their smokes to avoid the sniper and the 3 match trick they had.

The biggest short term consequence of smoking was if the soldier had been gassed, and the dreadful consequences of both on the lungs.

Documents

1   1901 Census return showing George Coward aged 12, living in Twerton, Bath

2   Private Coward's Decorations

The award of the "Clasps and Roses" to the 1914 Star was an award that needed to be claimed. The "clasp" is a bar inscribed "5 August. To 22 Nov. 1914" for which all those who served under fire during that period were eligible. Since the same ribbon is used with the 1914–15 Star, holders of the earlier award were permitted to wear a small silver rosette on their ribbon when the decoration itself is not worn, which is the "roses" in medals terminology. Men who served at this time were generally known as the "Old Contemptibles", and formed an association as such after the war. George's decorations were issued in February 1920.

The other two medals were the British War Medal and the Victory Medal. These are two standard awards for military service in the British Army in the Great War. Essentially the BWM was awarded if a man left his native shore for service, and the VM if he also served in a theatre of war.

The 1914 Star was reserved for those who served overseas prior to midnight on the 22/3 November, the officially recognised end of the First Battle of Ypres.

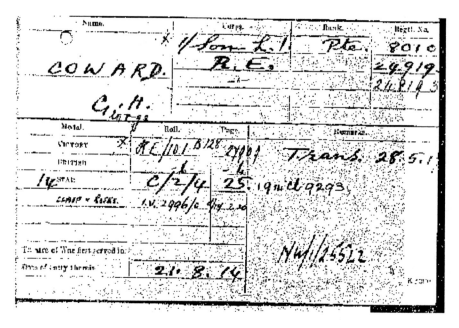

3   *A summary history of the 1st Battalion, Prince Albert's [Somerset Light Infantry] in 1914-18*

This was a battalion of the regular army that moved early to France as part of 11th Brigade of the 4th Division. It was involved in virtually every engagement from its arrival on 21 August 1914. This included the sharp fight at Le Cateau [26 August 1914], the subsequent trying retreat from Mons, the turnabout on the Marne, the advance to the Aisne and the start of entrenched warfare, and latterly the 1st Battle of Ypres. By the conclusion of the fighting at Ypres, in which the battalion had been engaged in the area of Ploegsteert wood near Armentières, it was no more than a remnant. Over the next few weeks the battalion was rebuilt, and received hundreds of men in new drafts.

The Division spent a wretched winter in the same area. The rudimentary trenches became flooded, and although there was no major fighting during the winter months many men were lost to snipers and occasional shellfire as both sides sought to improve the trenches, taking advantage of every patch of higher ground and carrying out much manual work on digging, riveting trench sides, baling water and installing pumps. On the 19 December, the battalion made an attack on the Birdcage position at Le Peterin hamlet near Ploegsteert that cost just over 100 casualties.

There was a most unusual break from this monotony at Christmas 1914, when the Brigade was amongst the units in the Armentières area where an unofficial truce led to many curious incidents. The story of the "Christmas Truce" has often been told. The Somersets were not in the line at the time, but news travelled fast to the billets and no doubt there was considerable excitement at this odd turn of events.

In the early evening of 22 April 1915, the enemy launched a surprise attack against the French forces holding the North side of the notorious Ypres Salient, employing the first time poison gas. On this occasion it was chlorine, issuing as a yellow white cloud discharging from cylinders and rolling across the fields near Langemarck. The defenders, not unnaturally, fled in disorder, and it was only incredible bravery by the neighbouring Canadian units that moved across to cover the gap that held the lines for the Allies. The attack was renewed over the next few days, and developed into a major engagement with both sides deploying reserves in a bitter struggle. This is known as the Second Battle of Ypres.

4th Division was amongst the formations rushed into the area to reinforce the line. 11th Brigade was deployed from St Jean towards Fortuin at 10.30pm on 25 April. There was a gap in the line and it was there job to fill it and hold it. Enemy infantry was beaten off a number of times whilst all units came under heavy fire from German artillery. Heavy shellfire fell on them for the next 8 days, and enemy attempts to advance were frequent. At many times, the enemy were in places only a matter of feet away. The physical and mental stress on the men is difficult to imagine. The battalions of the 11th Brigade retired under cover of a heavy mist only on May 3 1915.

After a brief rest the battalion moved back into the line, this time a little in the north of Mouse Trap farm [cynically called Shell Trap farm by the troops], and on May 13 faced a renewed enemy effort. At the peak, as an indication of the artillery fire the infantry had to endure, it was reckoned that 100 shells per minute were falling on Mouse Trap farm alone.

On this occasion gas was not used. The last time it had been employed was 24 April. Chlorine is not a persistent gas, and it would have dispersed, although no doubt there were pockets in shallow ground. The battlefield would of course also have been thick with smoke, cordite and fumes and other products of explosions.

The Division remained in the Ypres Salient for a considerable period and the battalion took no further part in any major action until mid 1916.

On July 1 1916 the battalion took part in the opening of the Somme Offensive. Attacking between Serre and Beaumont Hamel, the Somersets were swept by machine gun fire coming from the Redan Ridge and suffered heavy losses although small groups made it as far as the German front trench.

The Somersets were in action again on 12 October 1916, supporting the 12th Brigade's attack on Spectrum Trench, north of Lesboeufs, and was in the same area on October 23 in another fruitless attack, this time against Dewdrop and Spectrum trenches. These actions, undertaken in atrocious weather, formed part of the battle of Transloy Ridge.

Throughout the Somme offensive, the battalion lost many men, not only as battle casualties but to the terrible conditions of weather and stress.

The Division was heavily engaged in the Battle of Arras in April 1917 and it was shortly after this that George transferred to the RE.

Later in the year, in September and October 1917, the 4th Division took part in the later stages of the 3rd Battle of Ypres, which is more often called Passchendaele, and also went on to see a great deal of fighting in 1918.

George Coward was one of the special reservists called up at the start of the war. Most of these went into the 1st Battalion. Records suggest there were about 700 of these and that they put the Battalion up to full strength of just over 1000. This was at Goojerat Barracks at Colchester at the time, though a small detachment of regulars was at Felixstowe.

The 1st Battalion Muster Roll:
  Private G Coward
  a.   Regimental Number: 8010.
  b.   Went out to France with the Battalion 21st August 1914.
  c.   Reported missing 2nd November 1914 and to England on the same date.
  d.   Admitted Home Hospital Edinburgh as wounded 3rd November 1914.
  e.   Embarked for France 2nd June 1915.
  f.   Rejoined the Battalion 4th June 1915.
  g.   To 11 Infantry Brigade HQ 3rd August 1915.
  h.   Transferred to Royal Engineers (4 Division Signal Company) 28th May 1917.

Postscript

George Coward's Son in Law, Donald Martin, has briefly told me what happened to George after the War, and given a character description.

"He was a likeable person and saw humour in everything he did". These qualities must have been invaluable during the War.

He was employed as a crane driver by Stothert and Pitt, one of Bath's main engineering companies. He was caught up in the unemployment of the 1920's, and did gardening to earn some cash, as well as growing food for his own family. He went to a local pub called the Hop Pole and liked pub games.

At the conclusion of the Great War he became a member of the "Old Contemptible Association", and was active in the British Legion throughout his life.

George died in 1962.

George Coward at his daughter Irene's wedding in Bath in 1947

Printed in the United Kingdom
by Lightning Source UK Ltd.
115260UKS00001B/121-132